Unique Mandalas

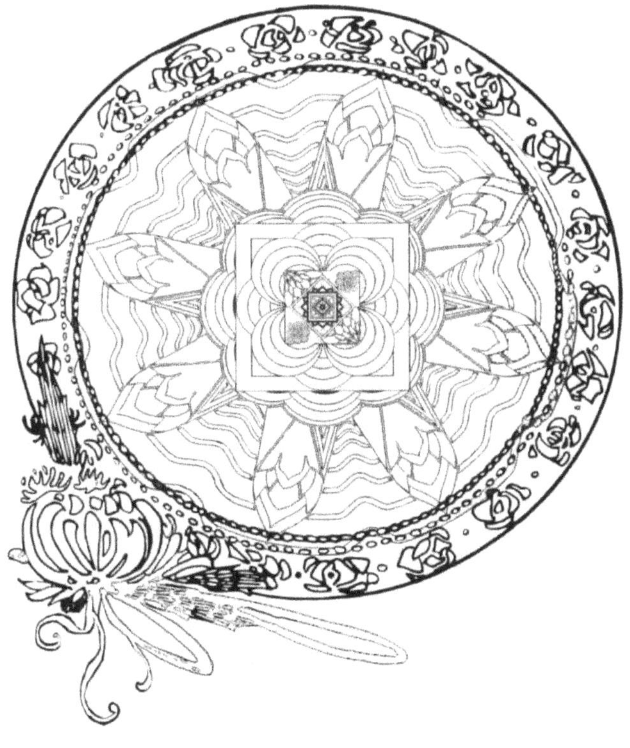

Created by: Trueheart Designs

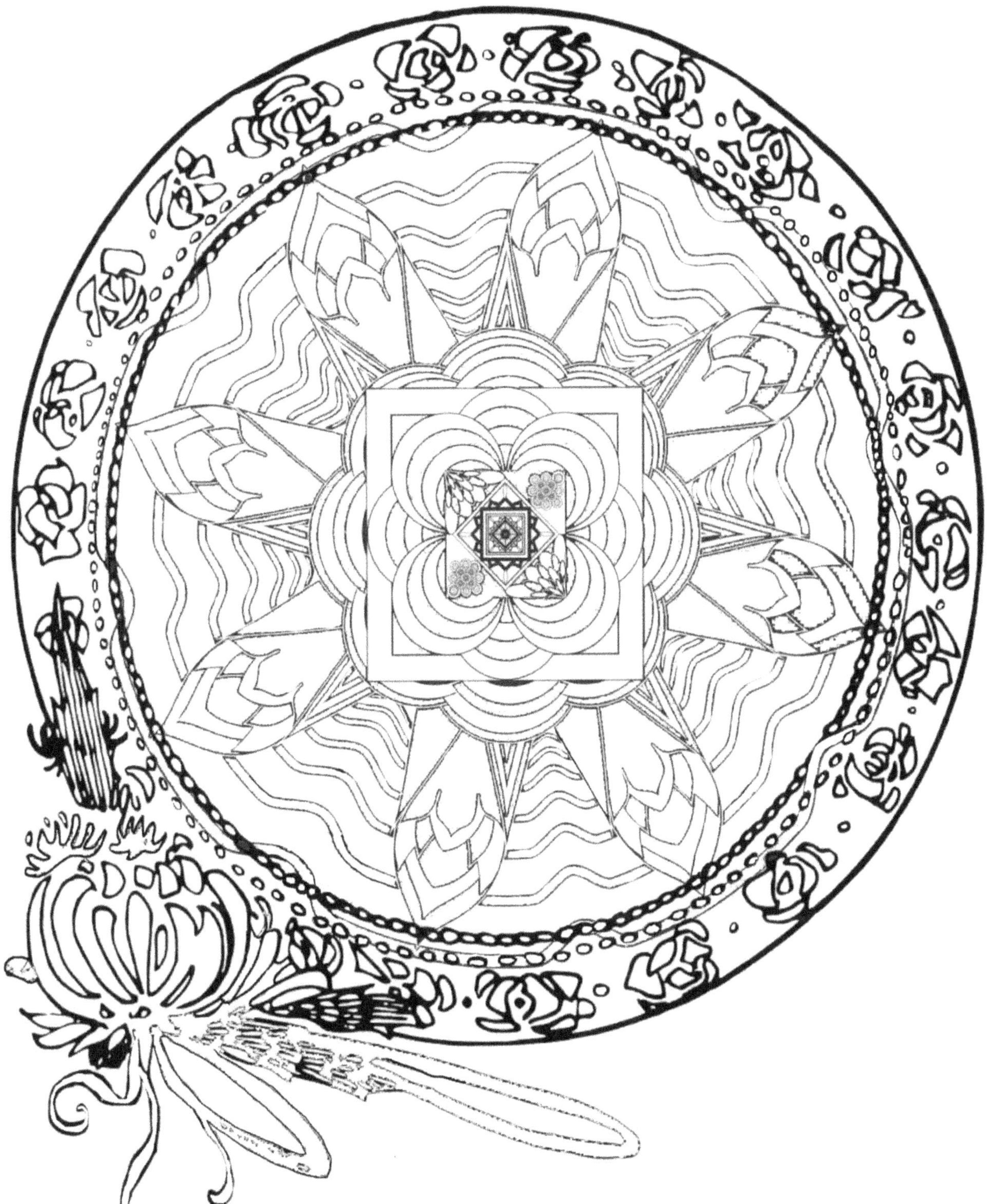

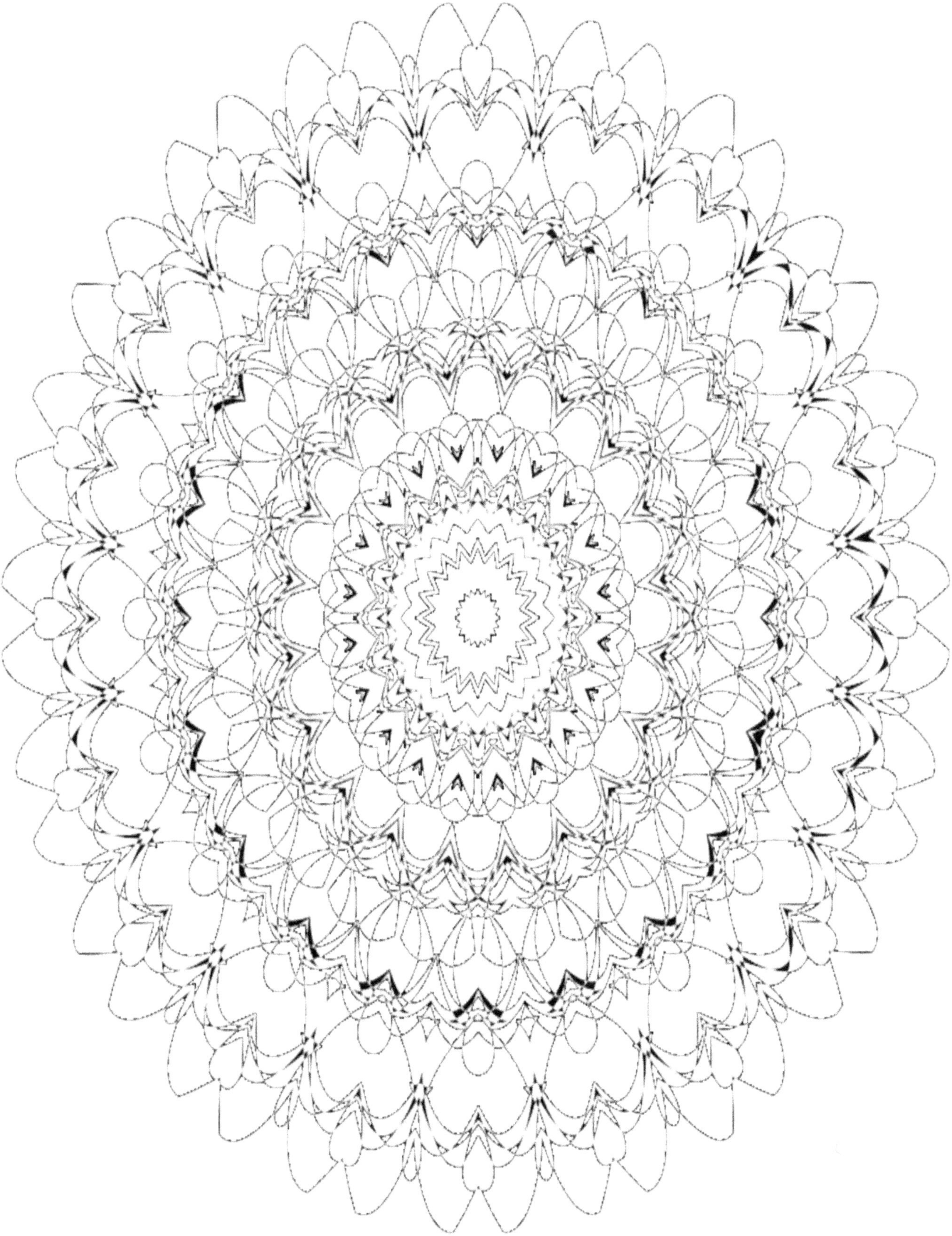

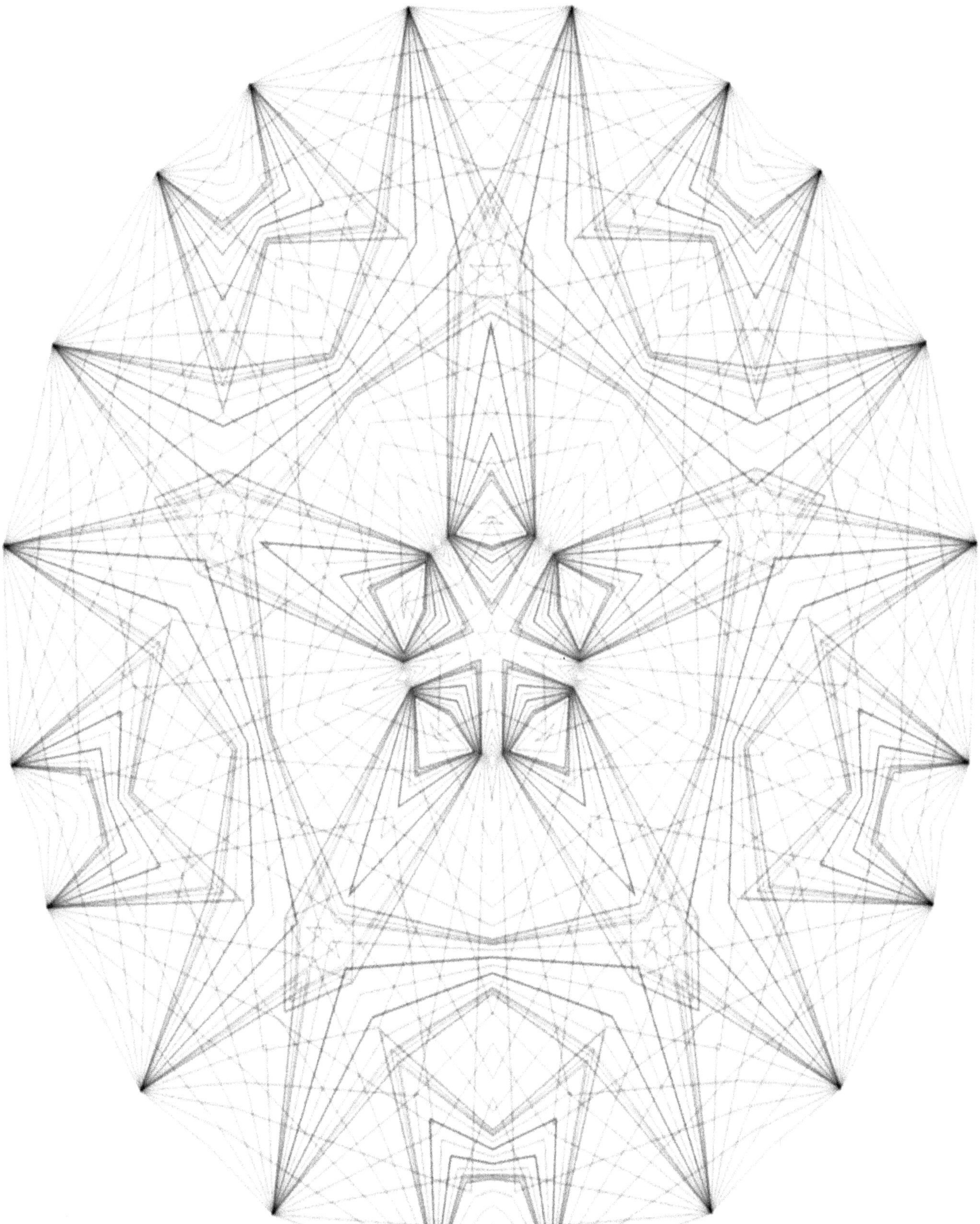

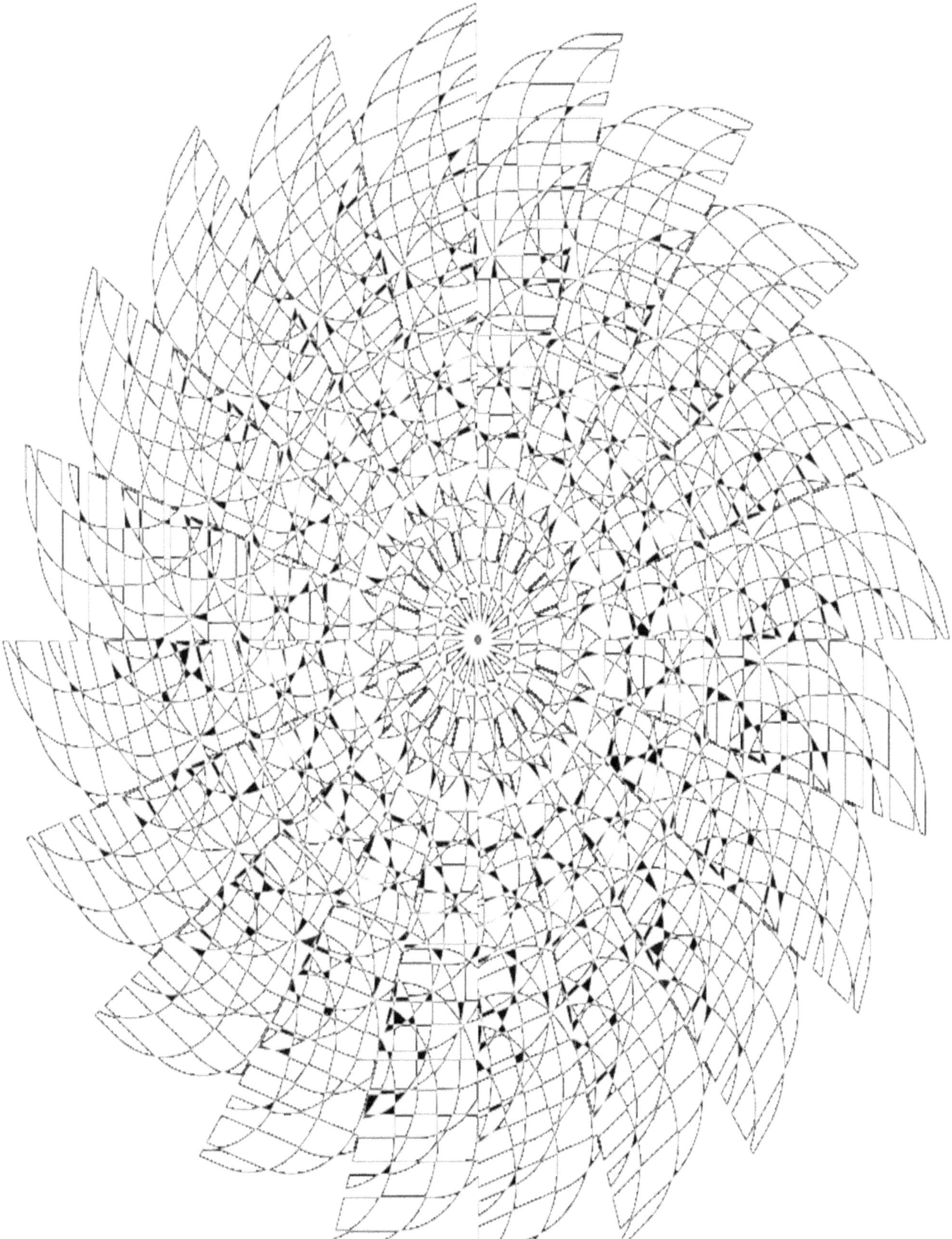

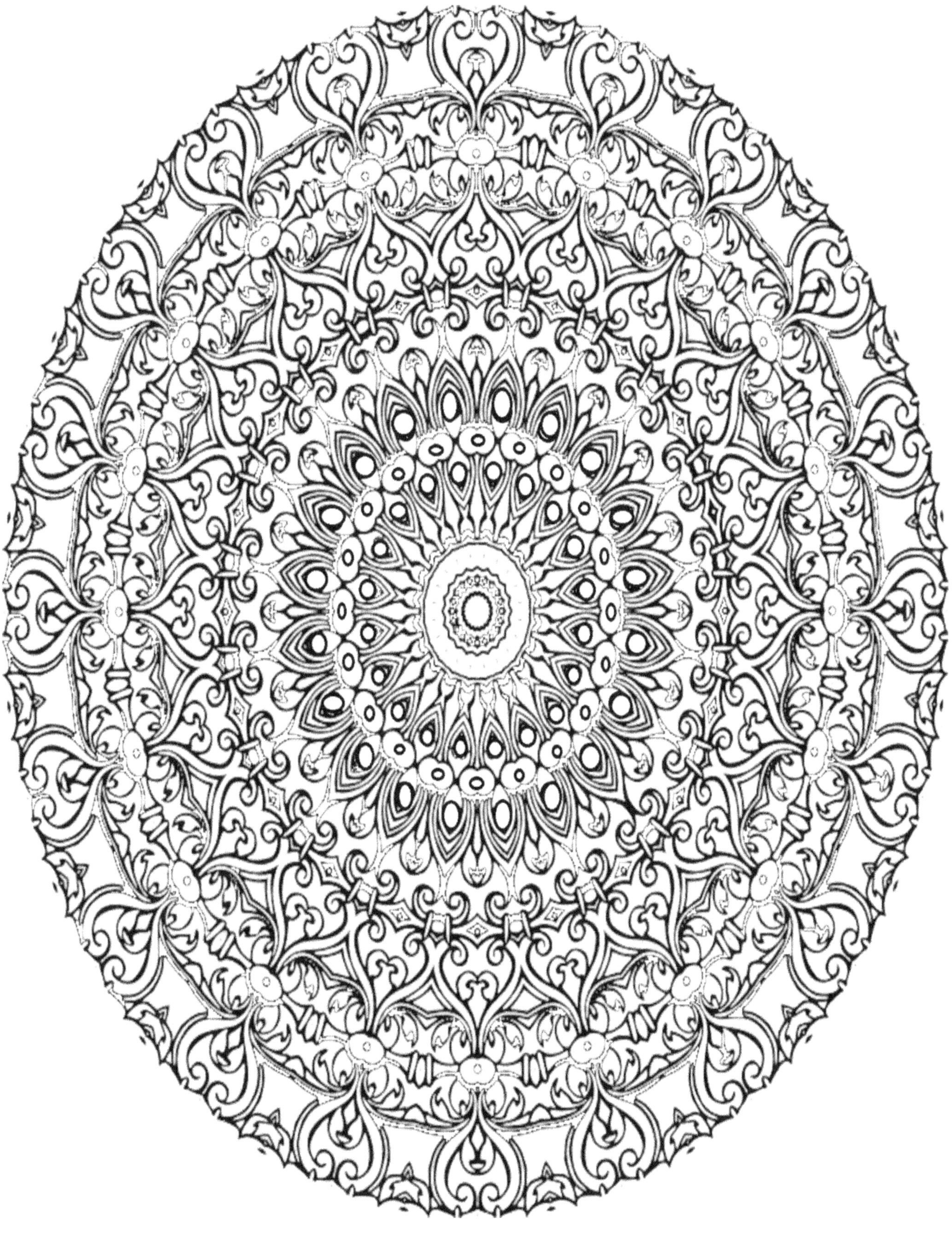

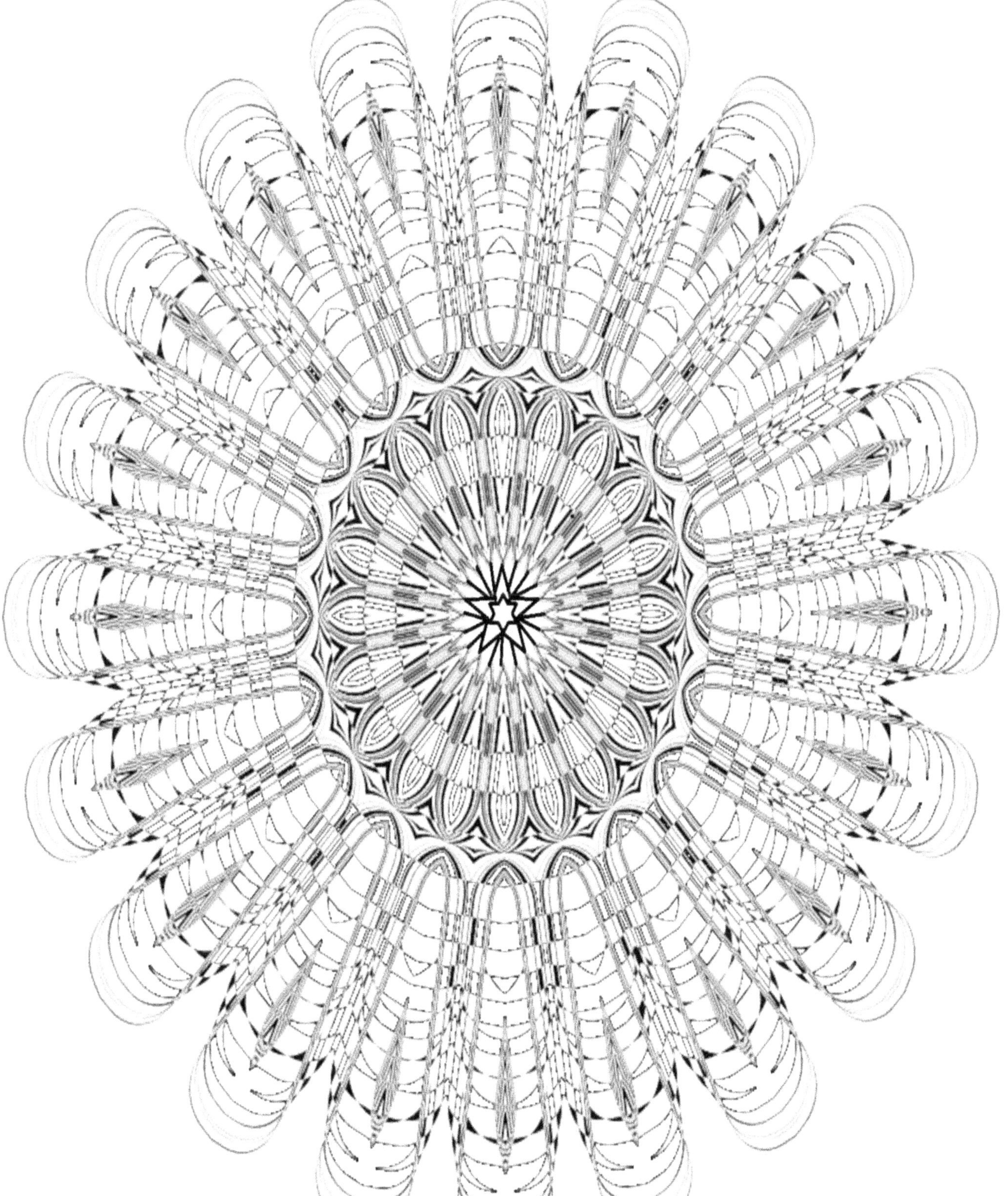

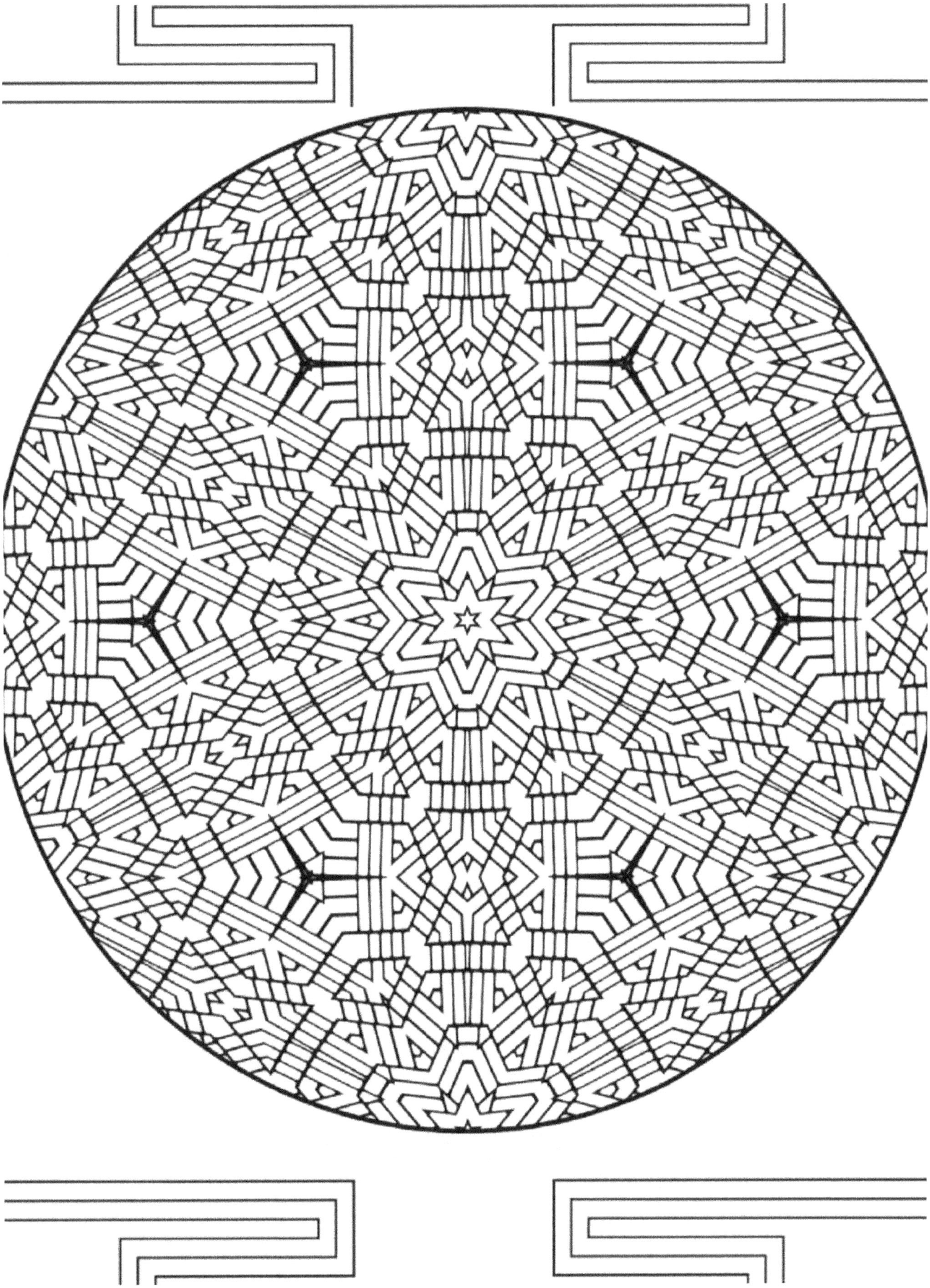

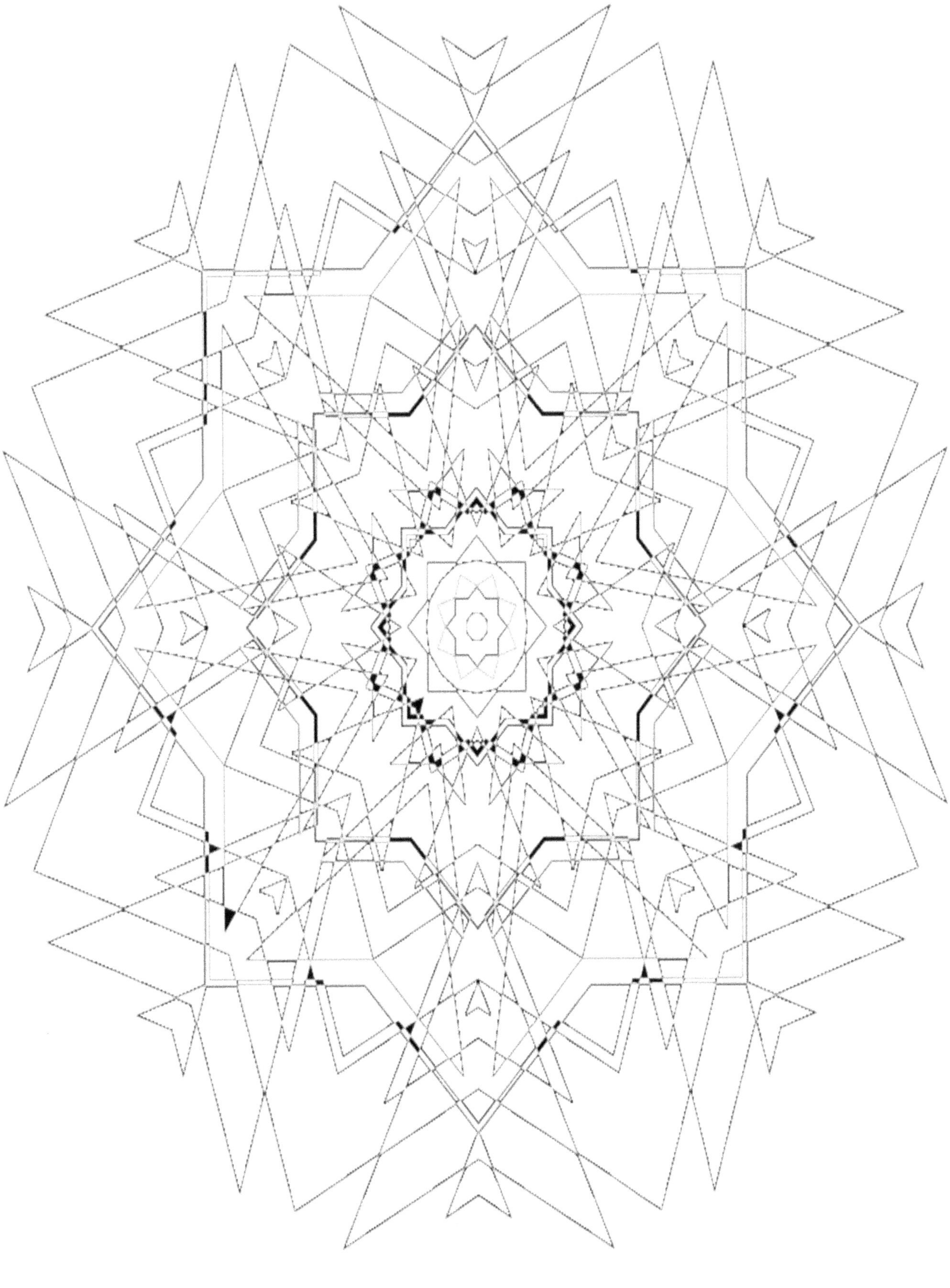

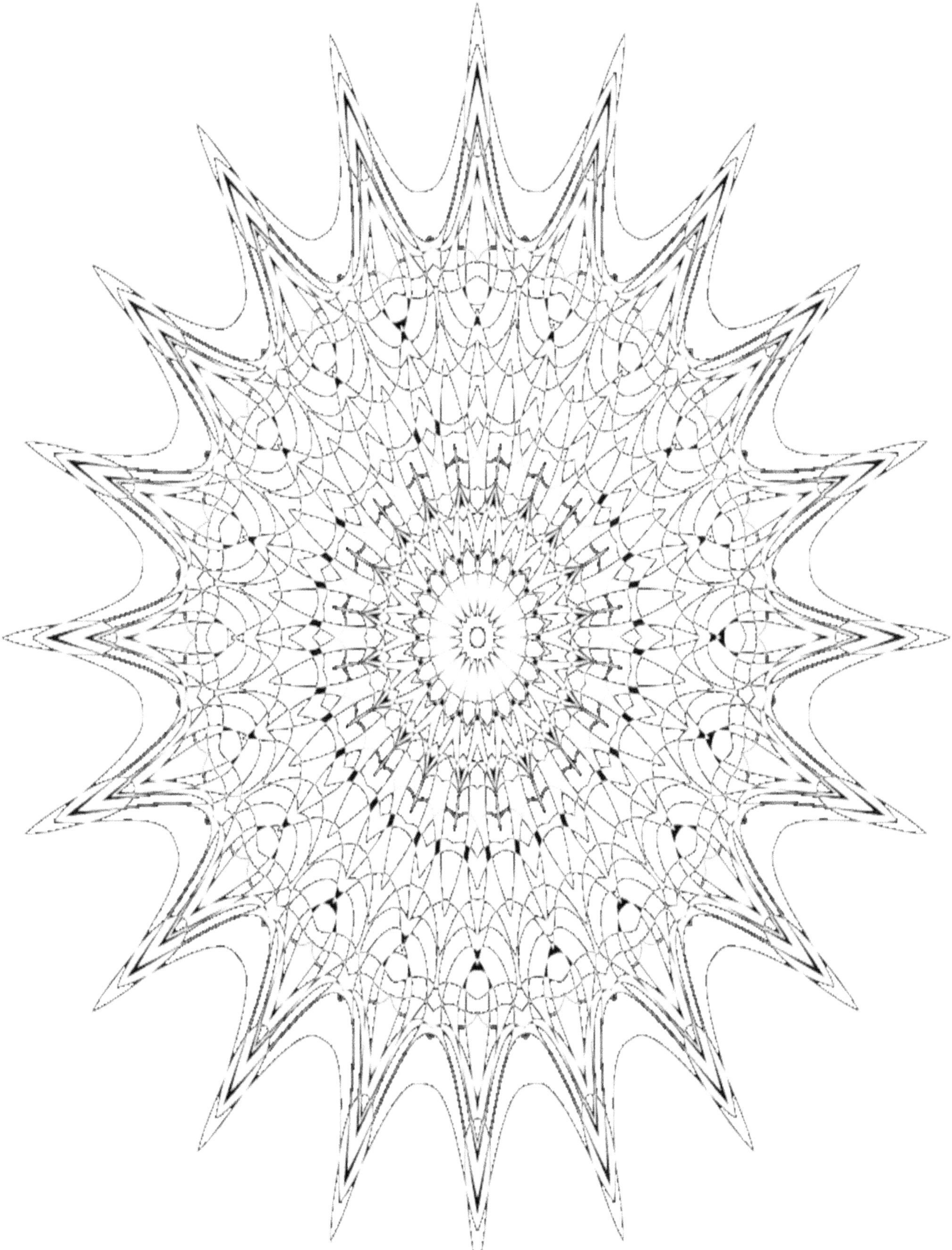

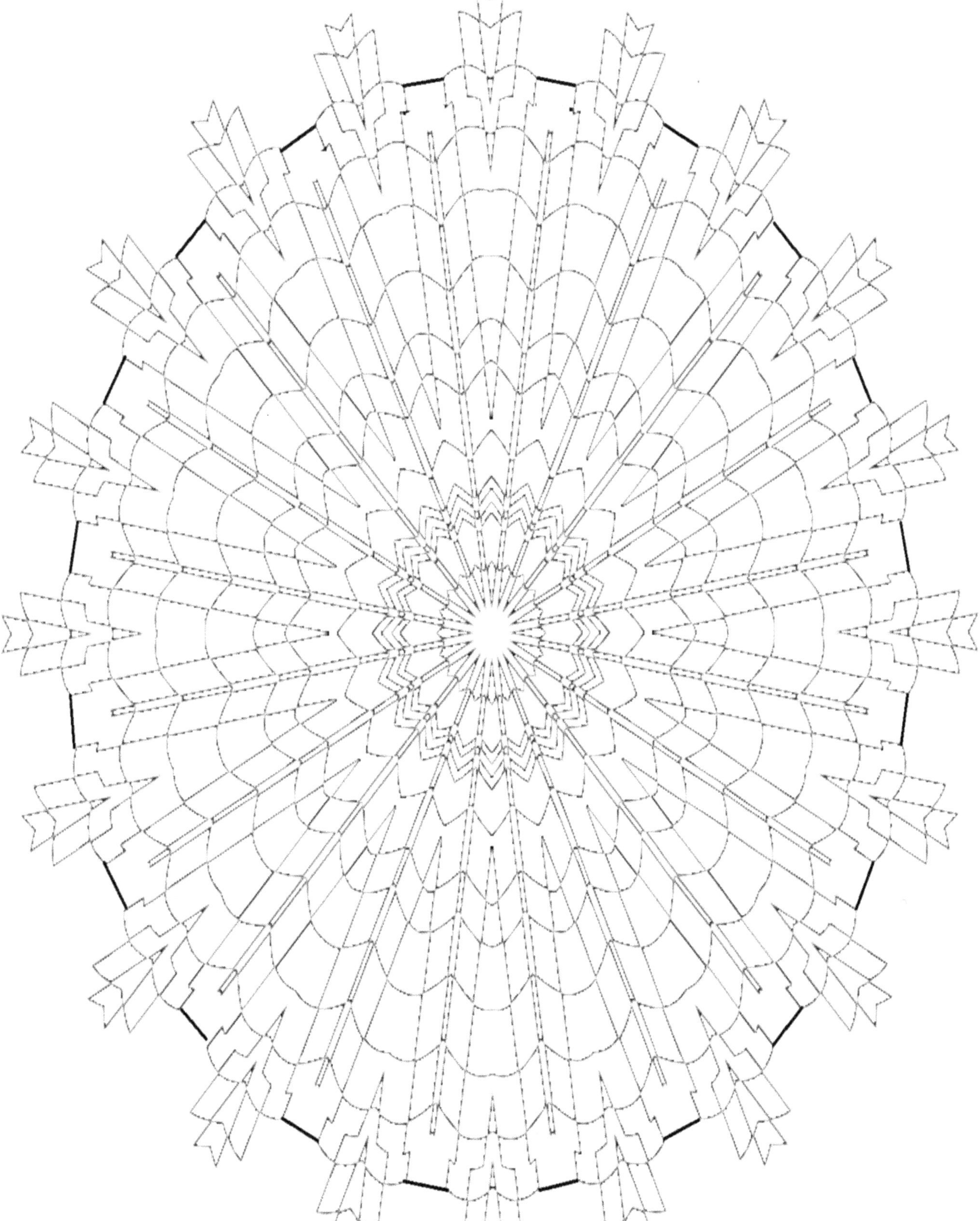

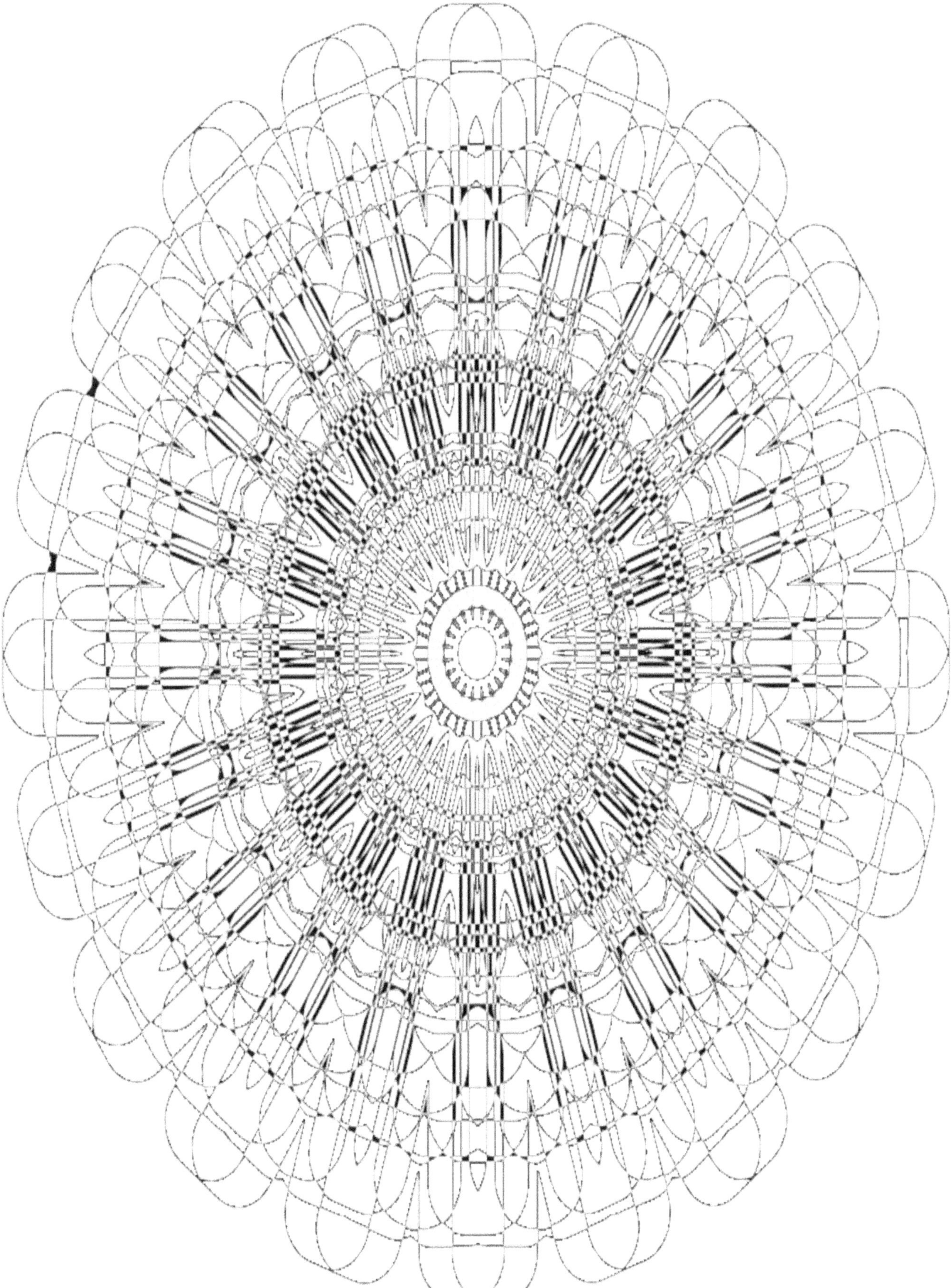

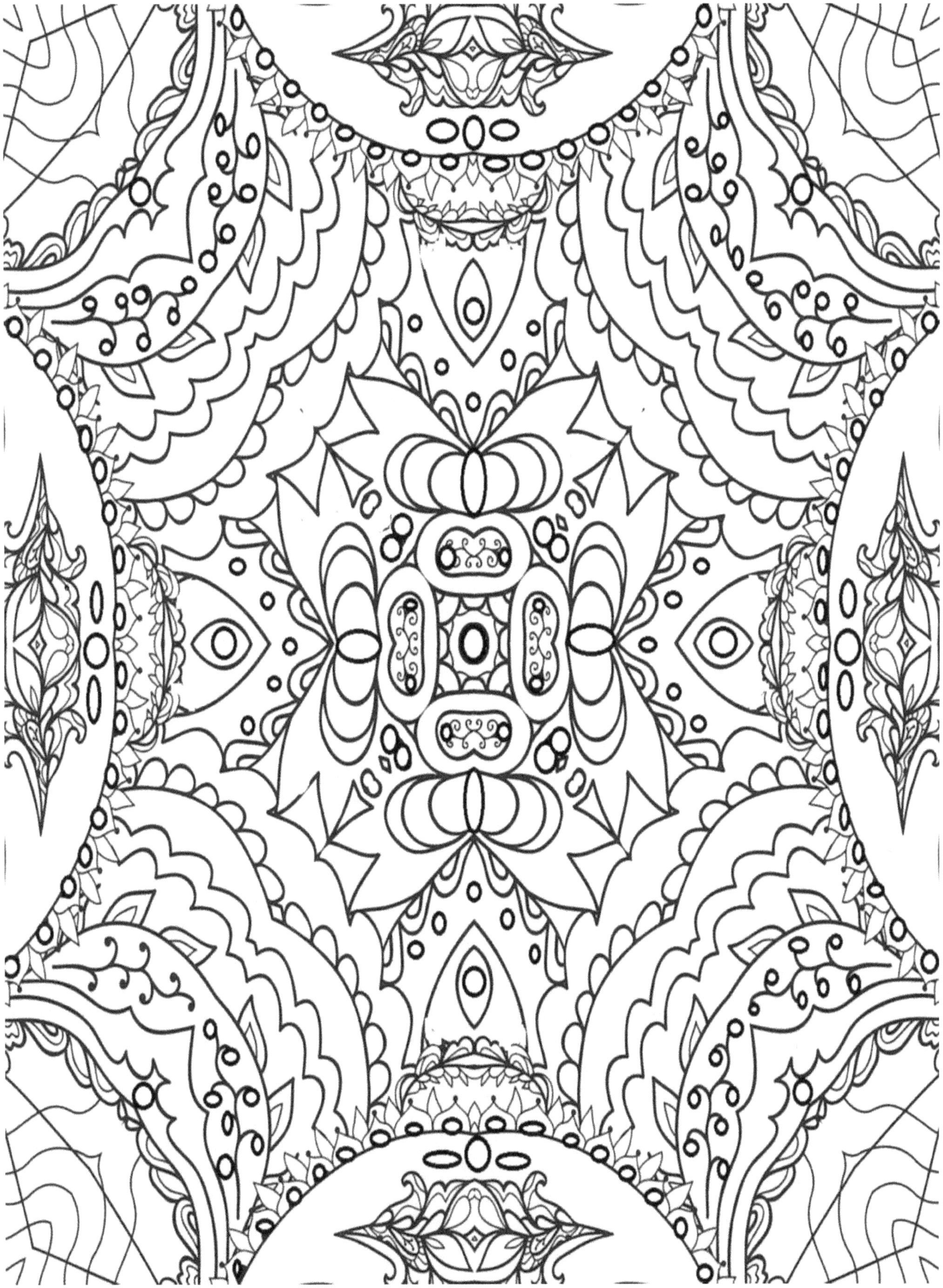

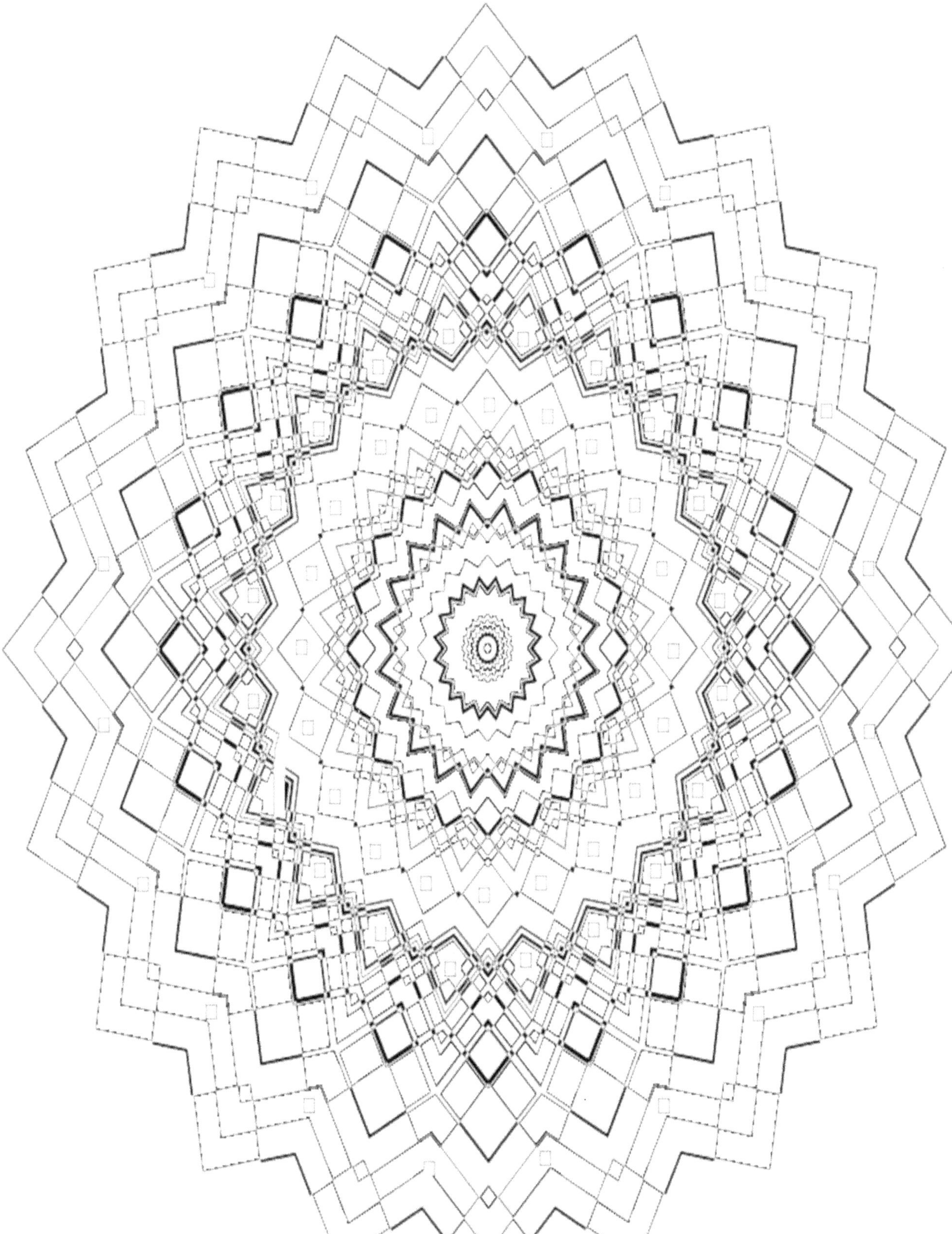

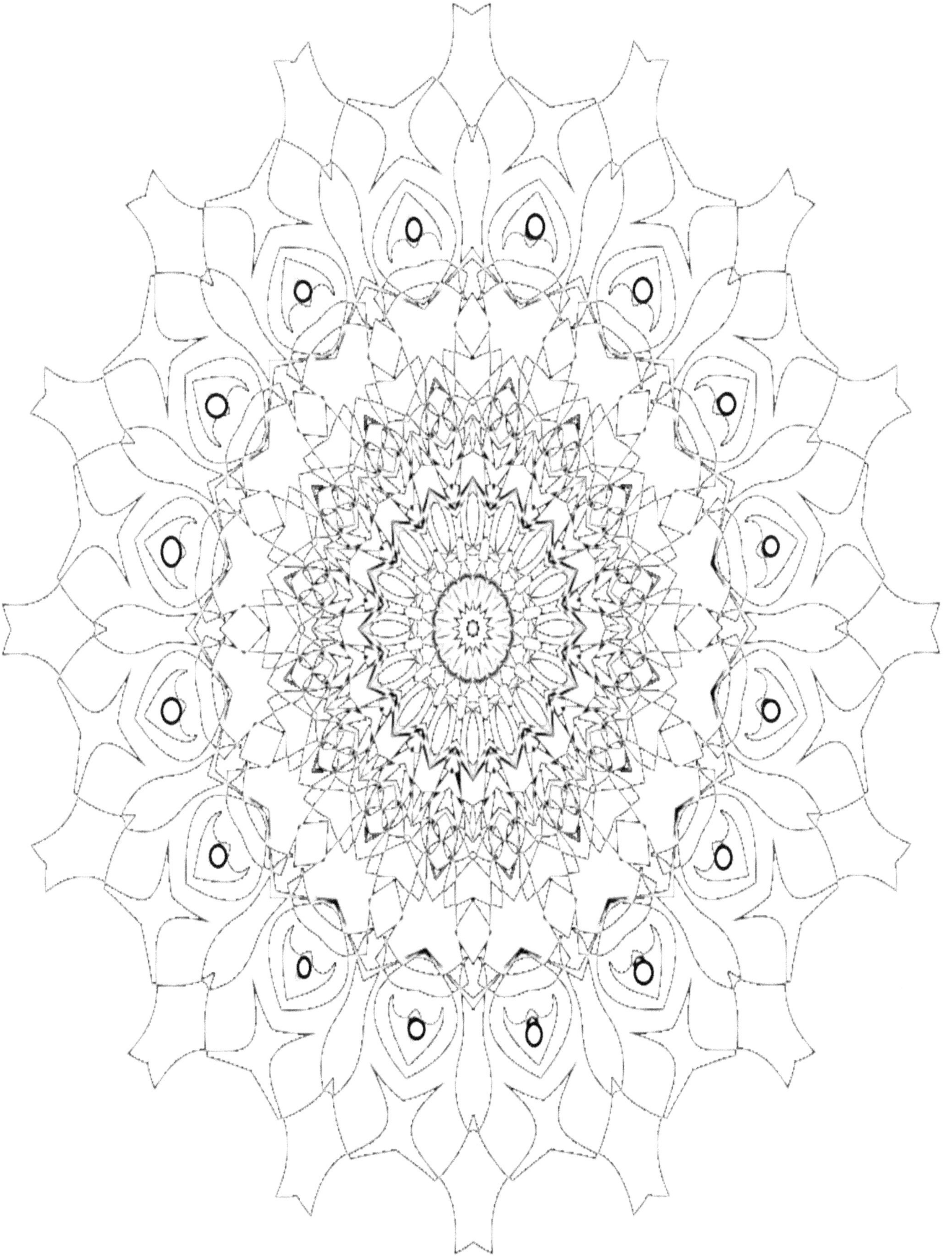

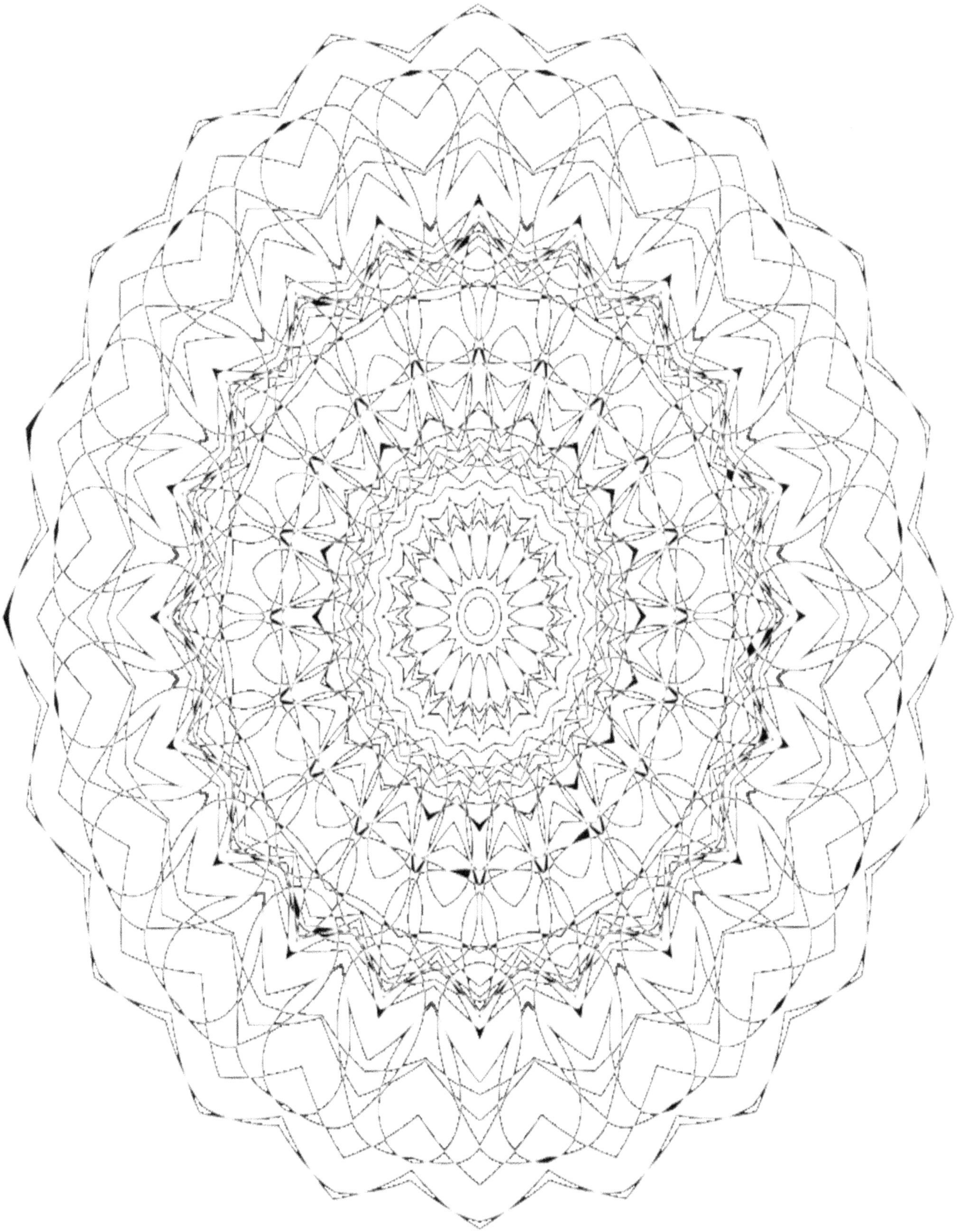

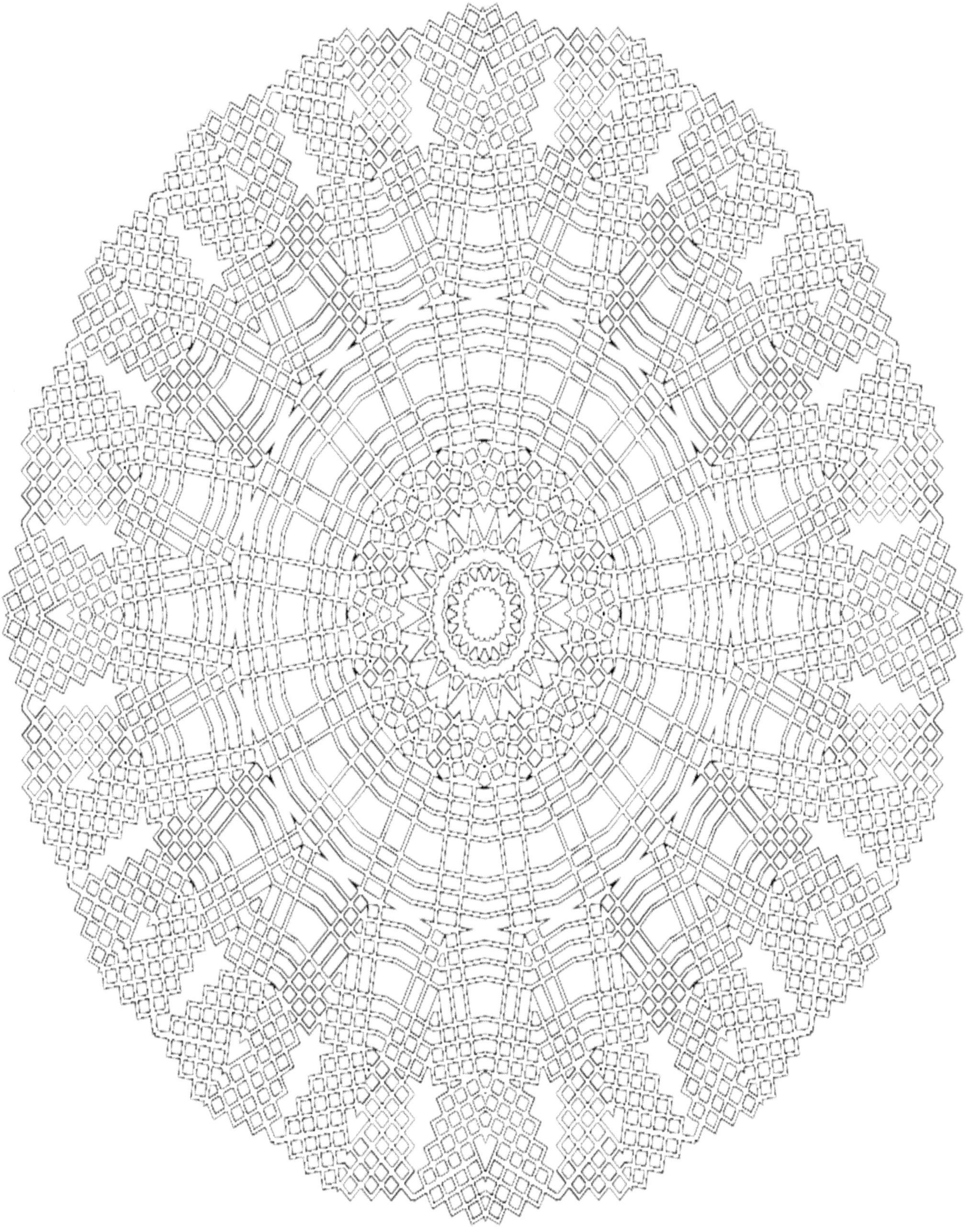

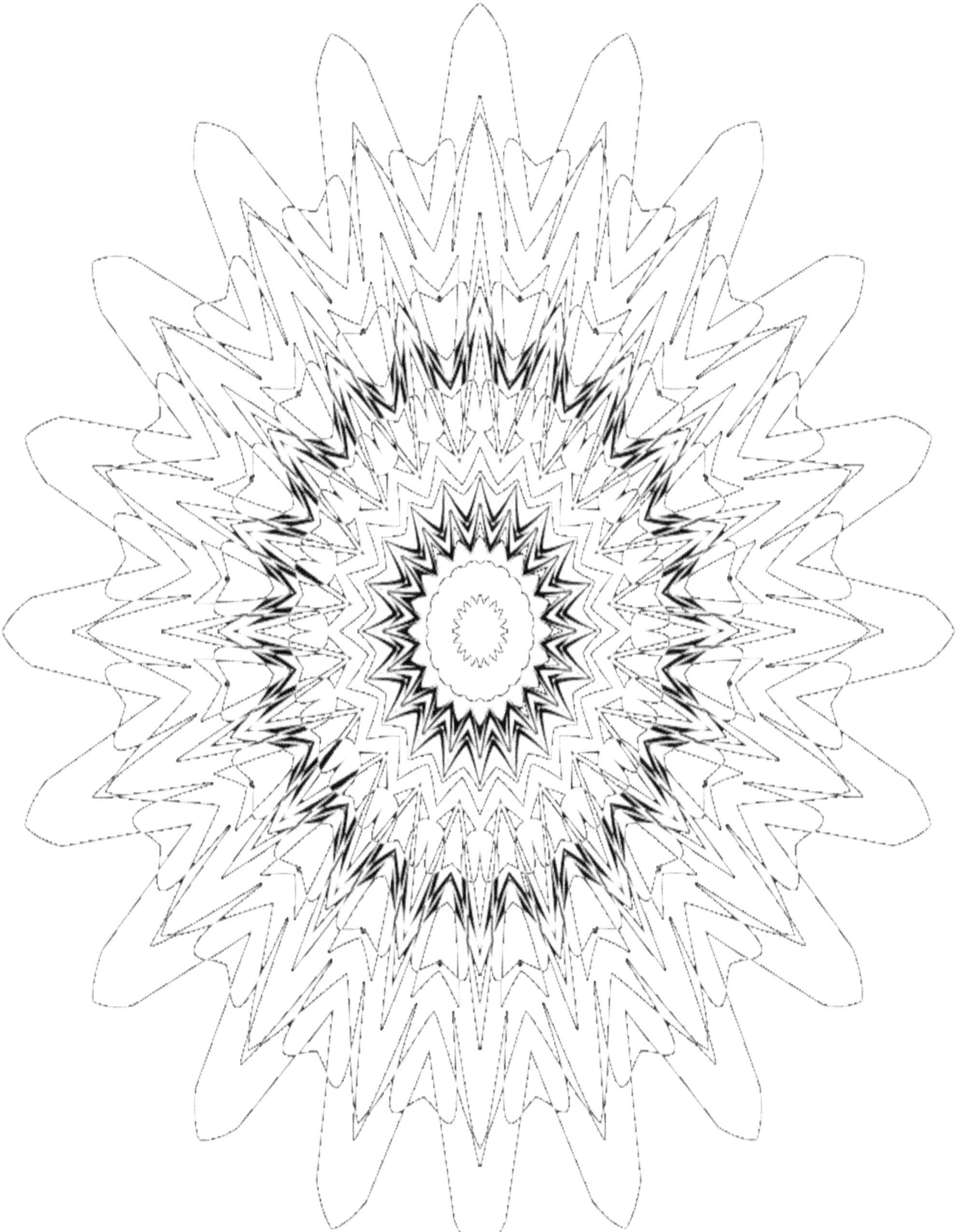

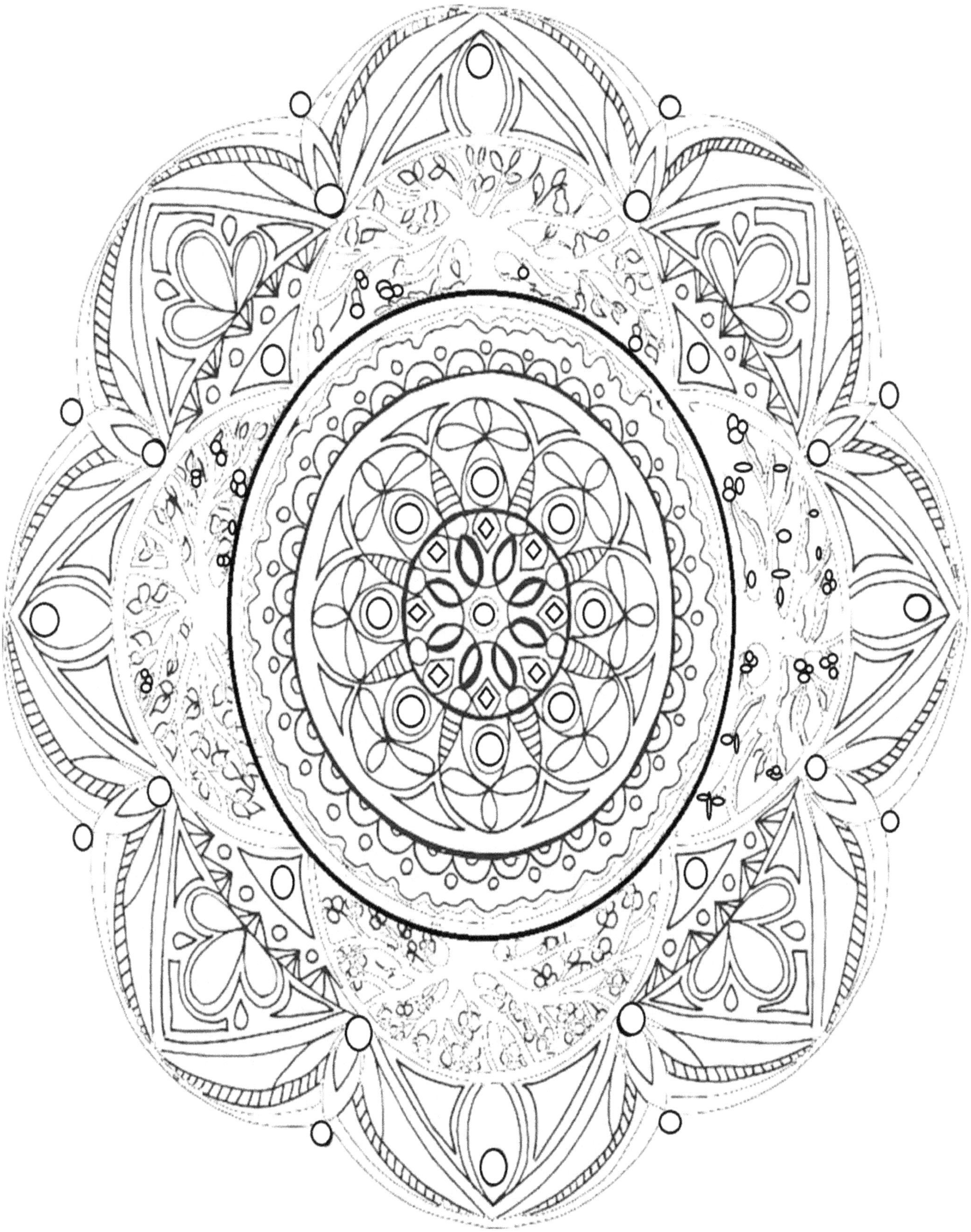

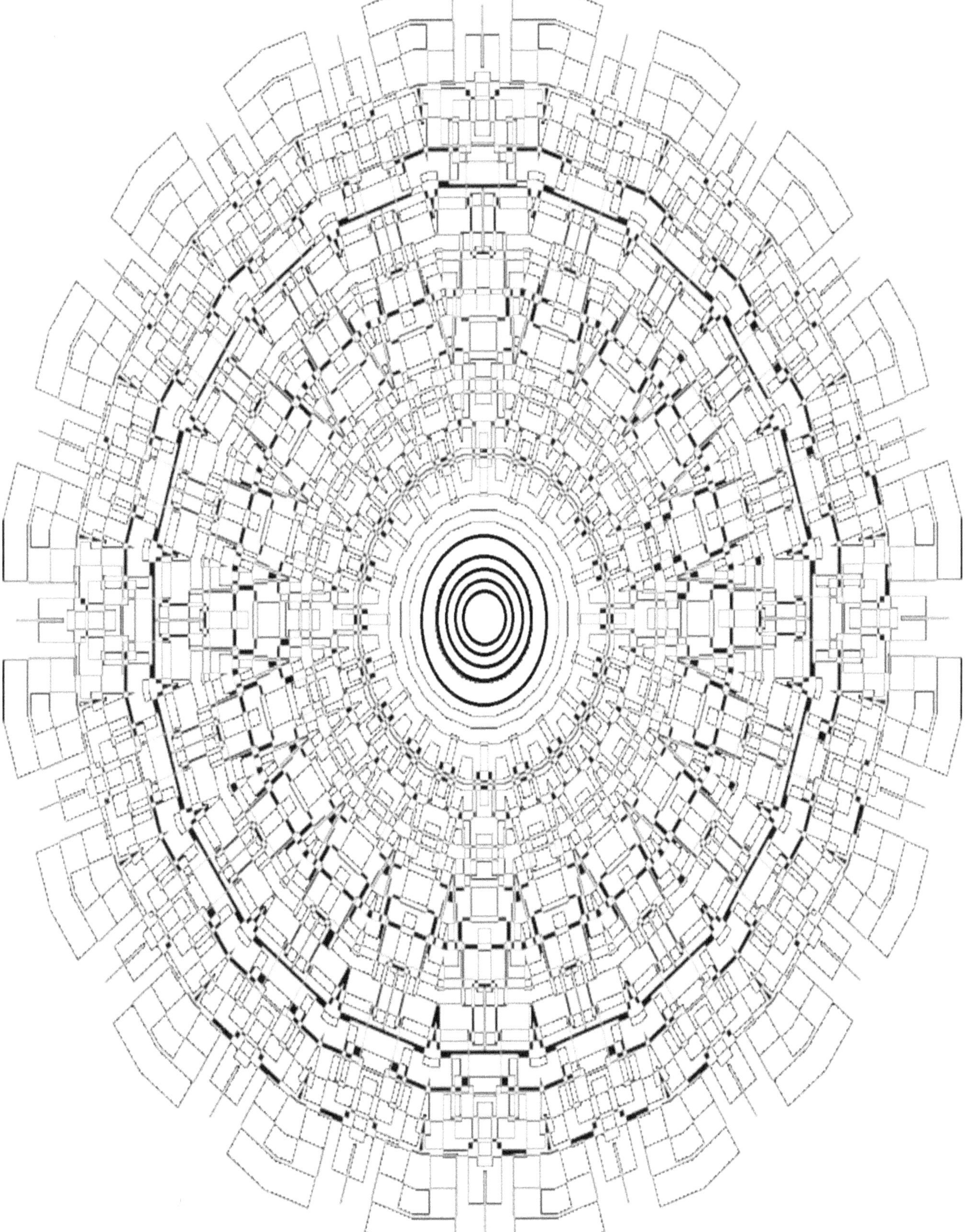

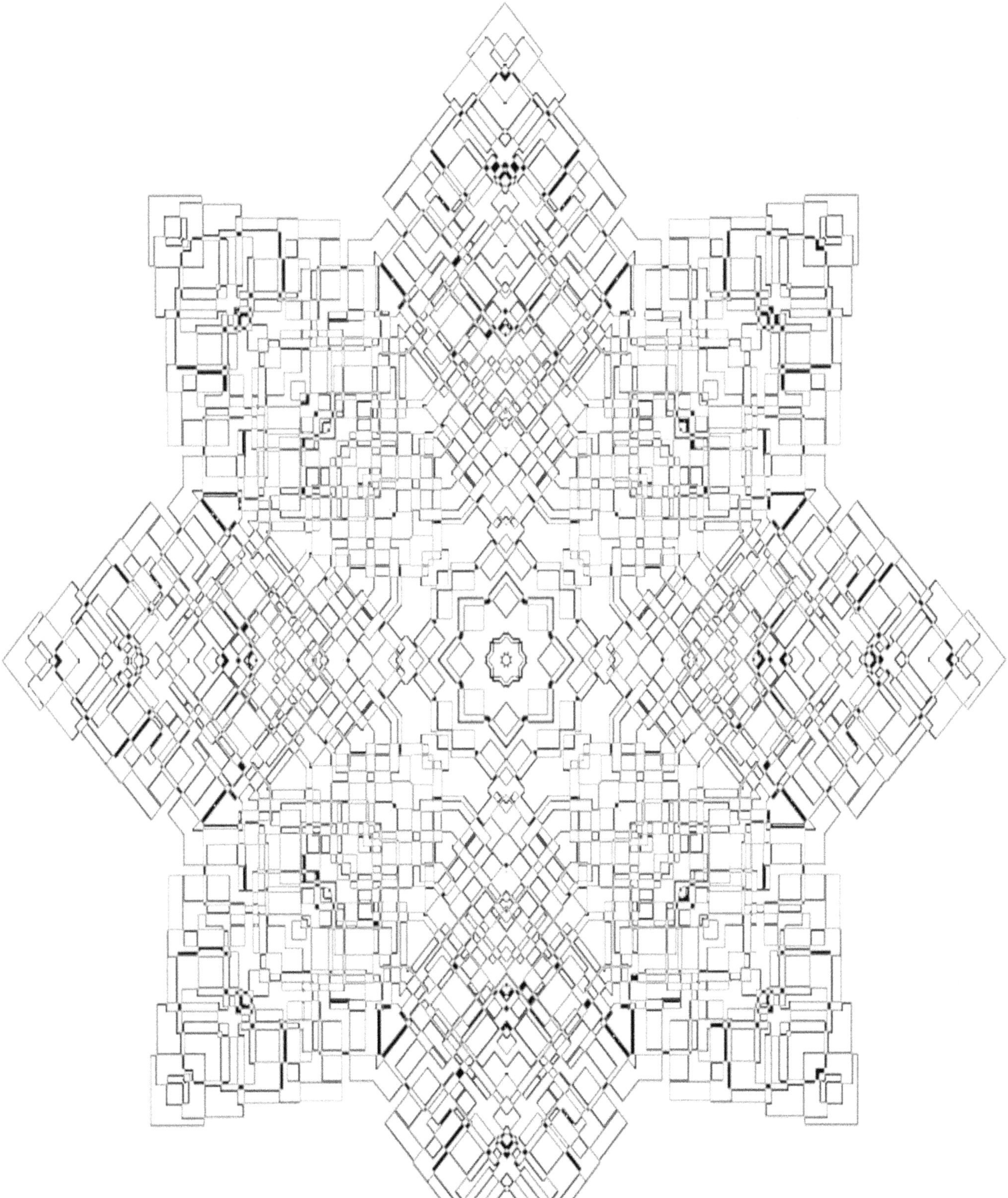

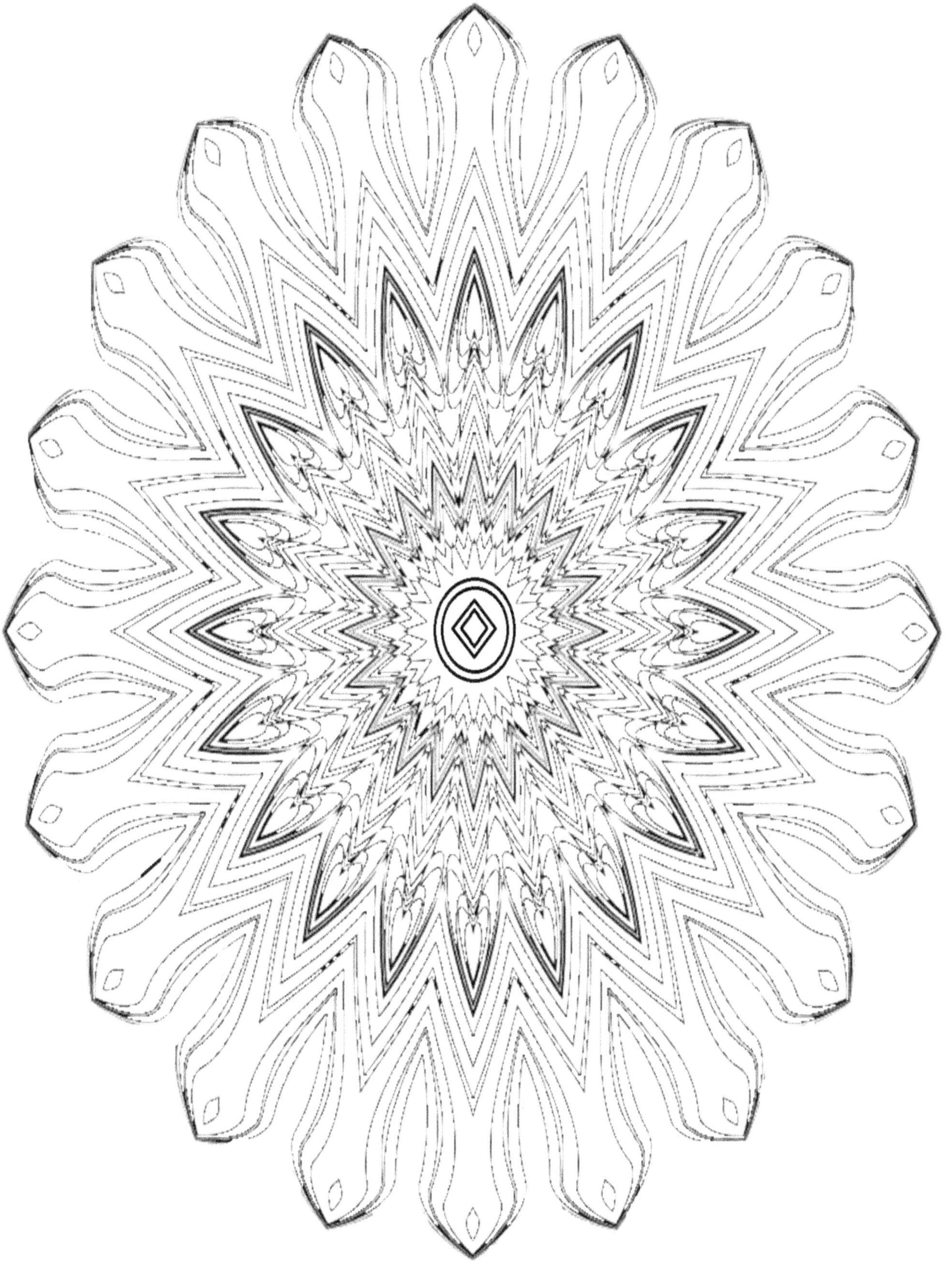

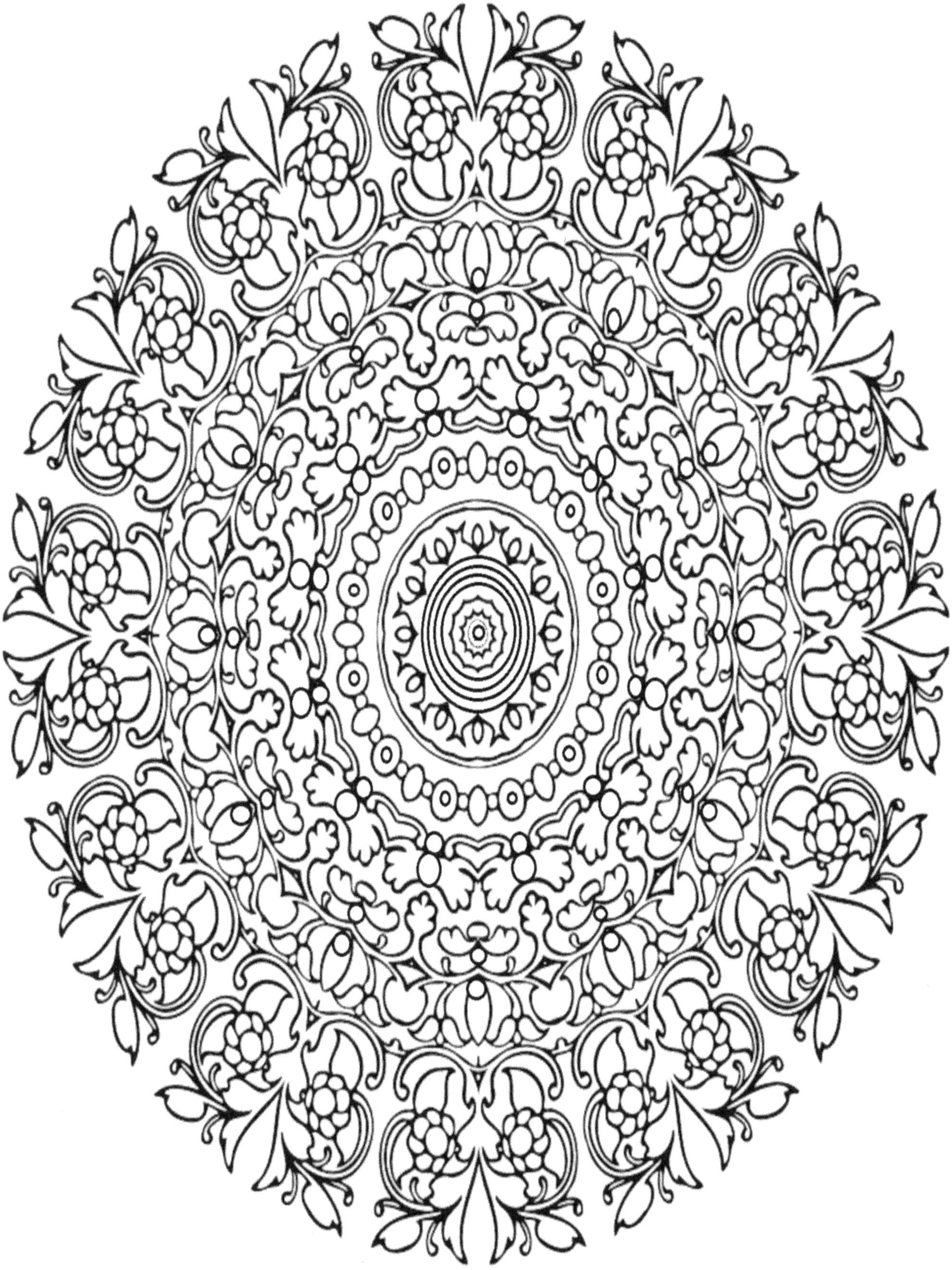

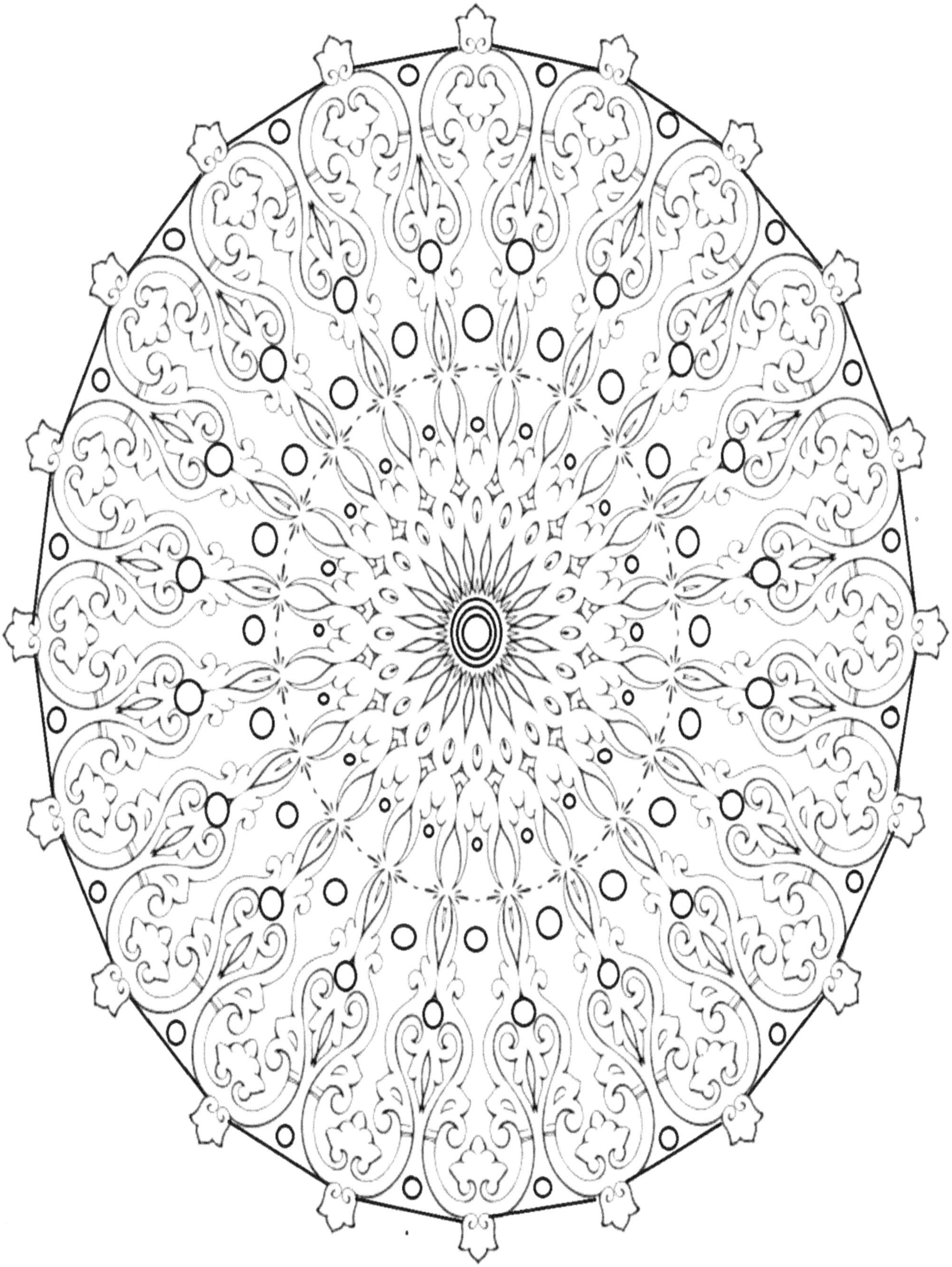

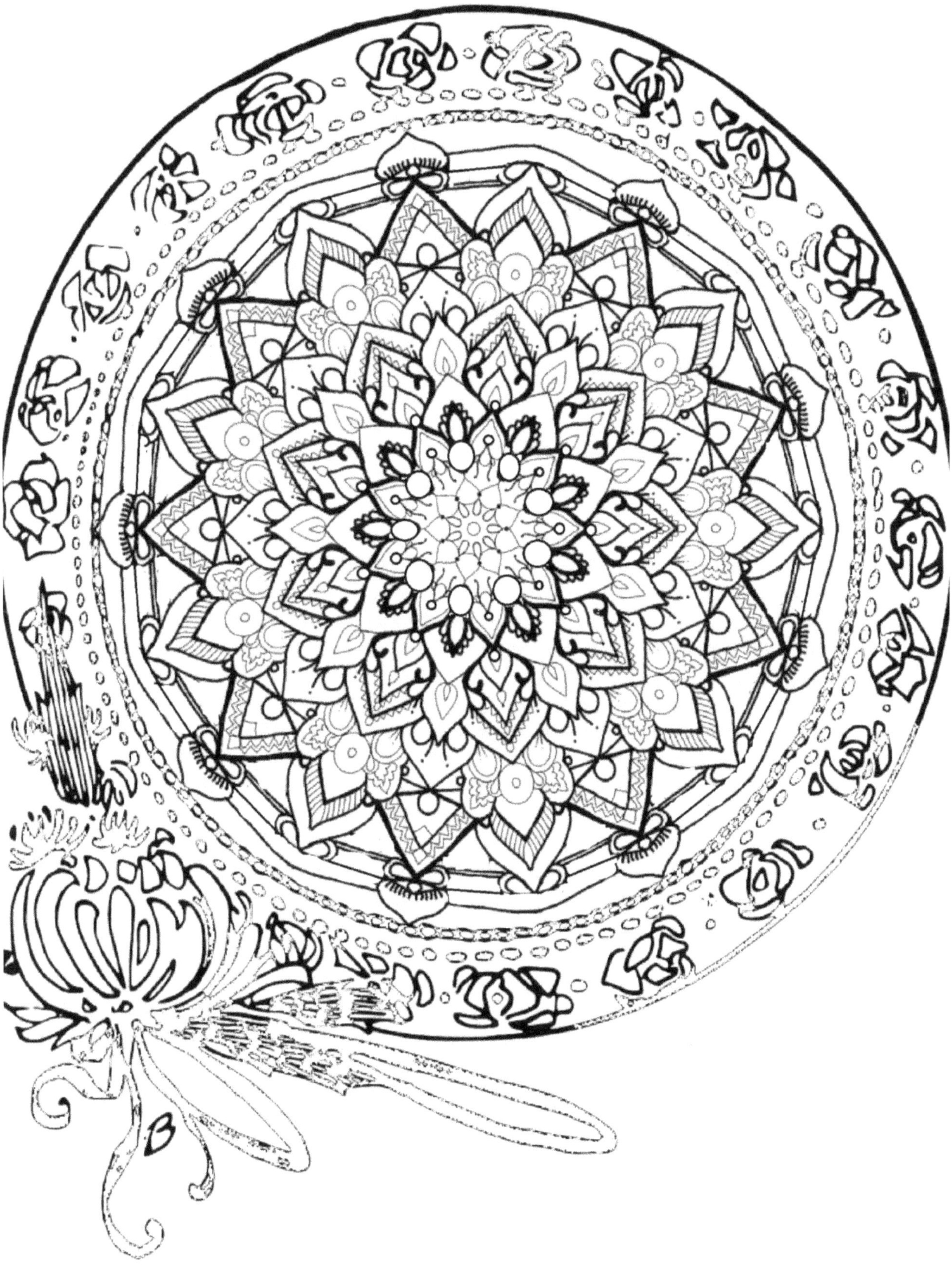

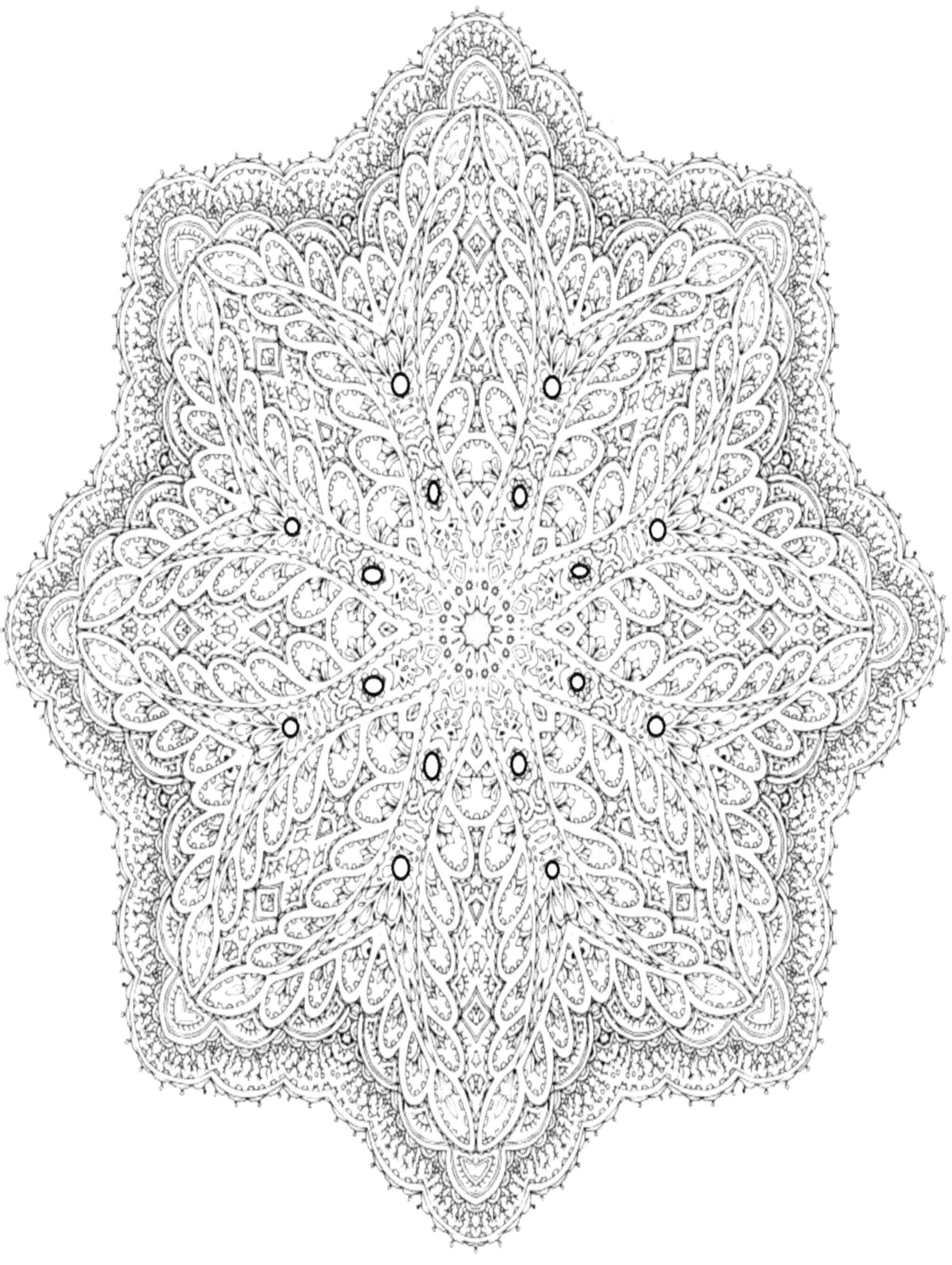

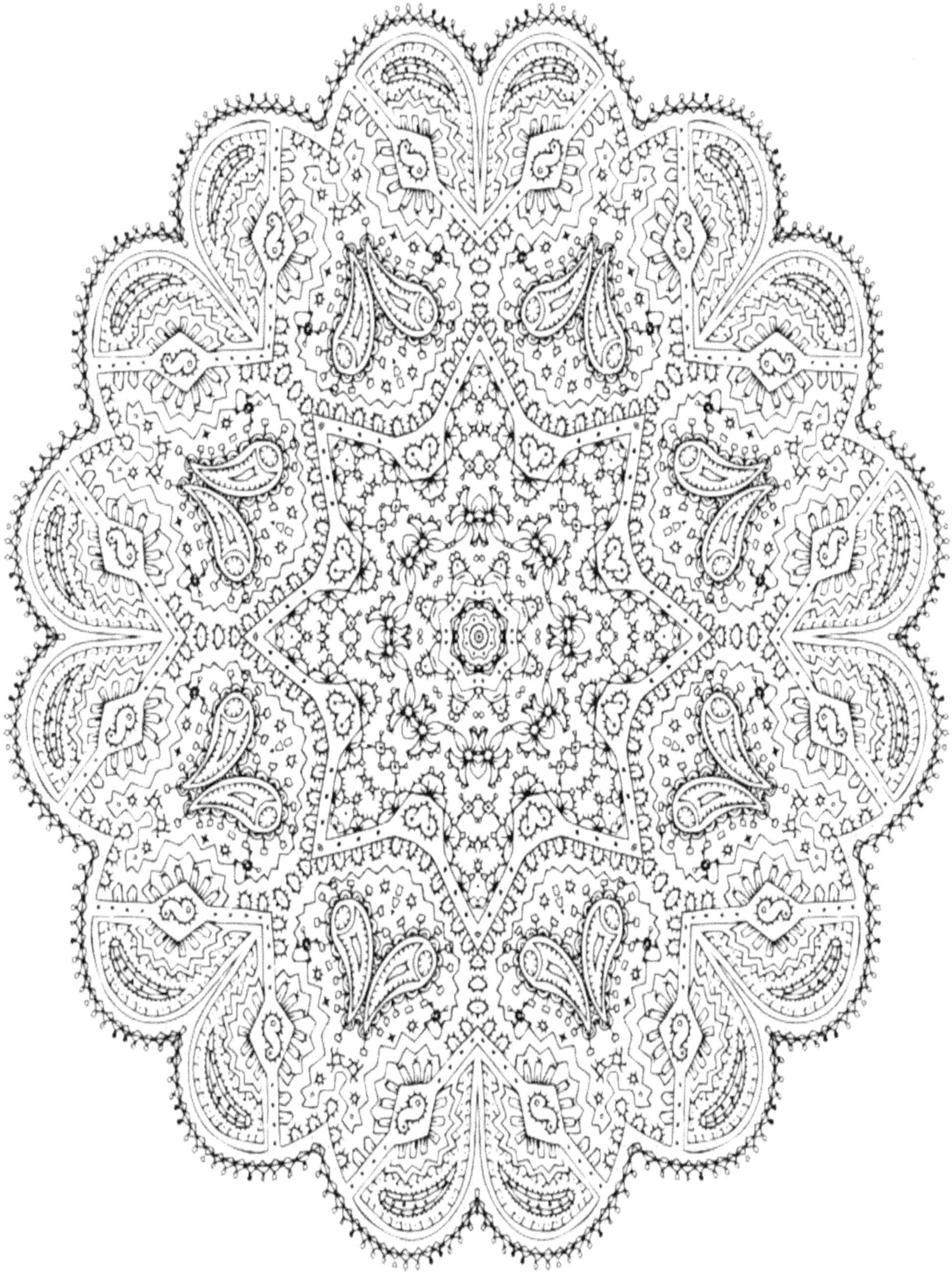

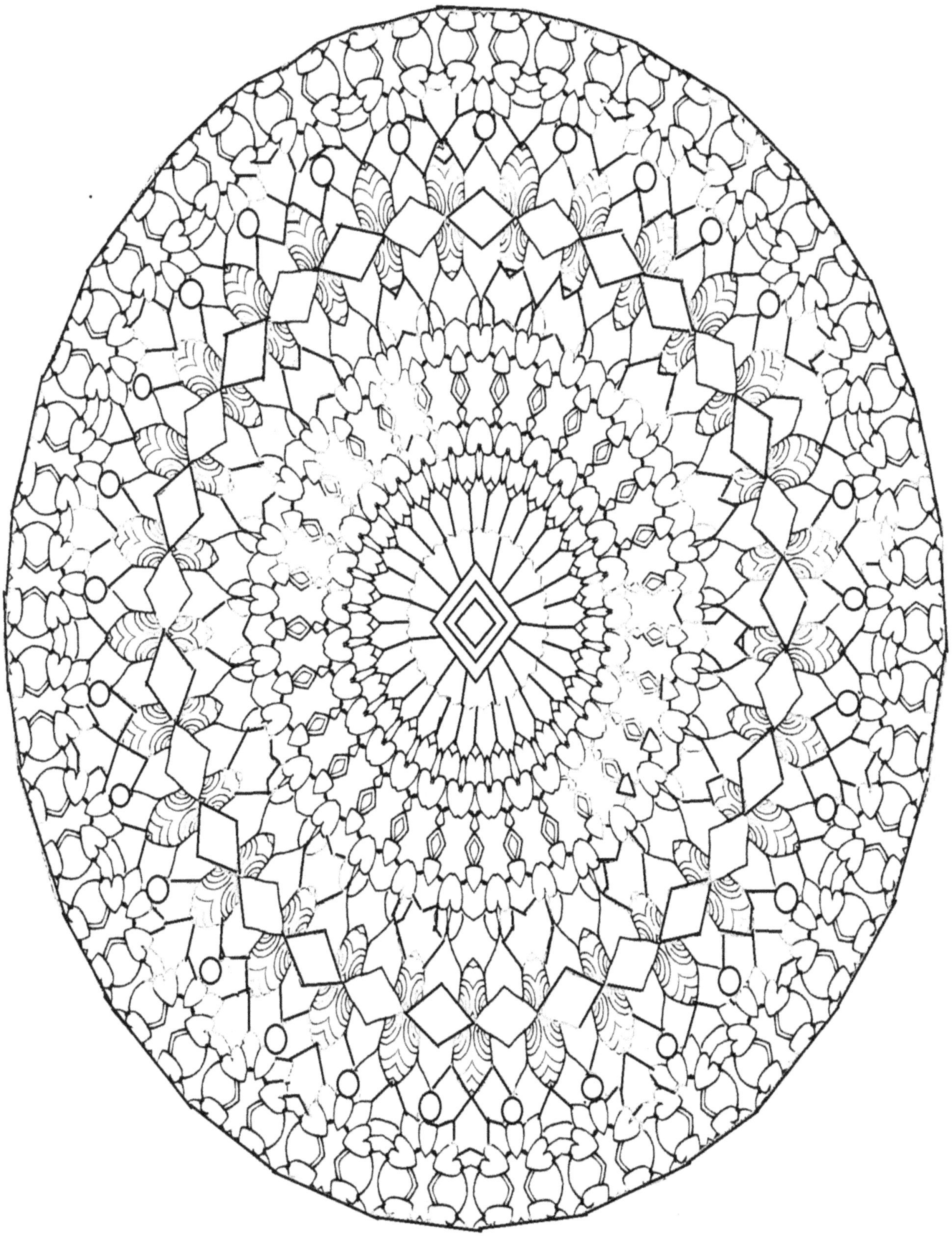

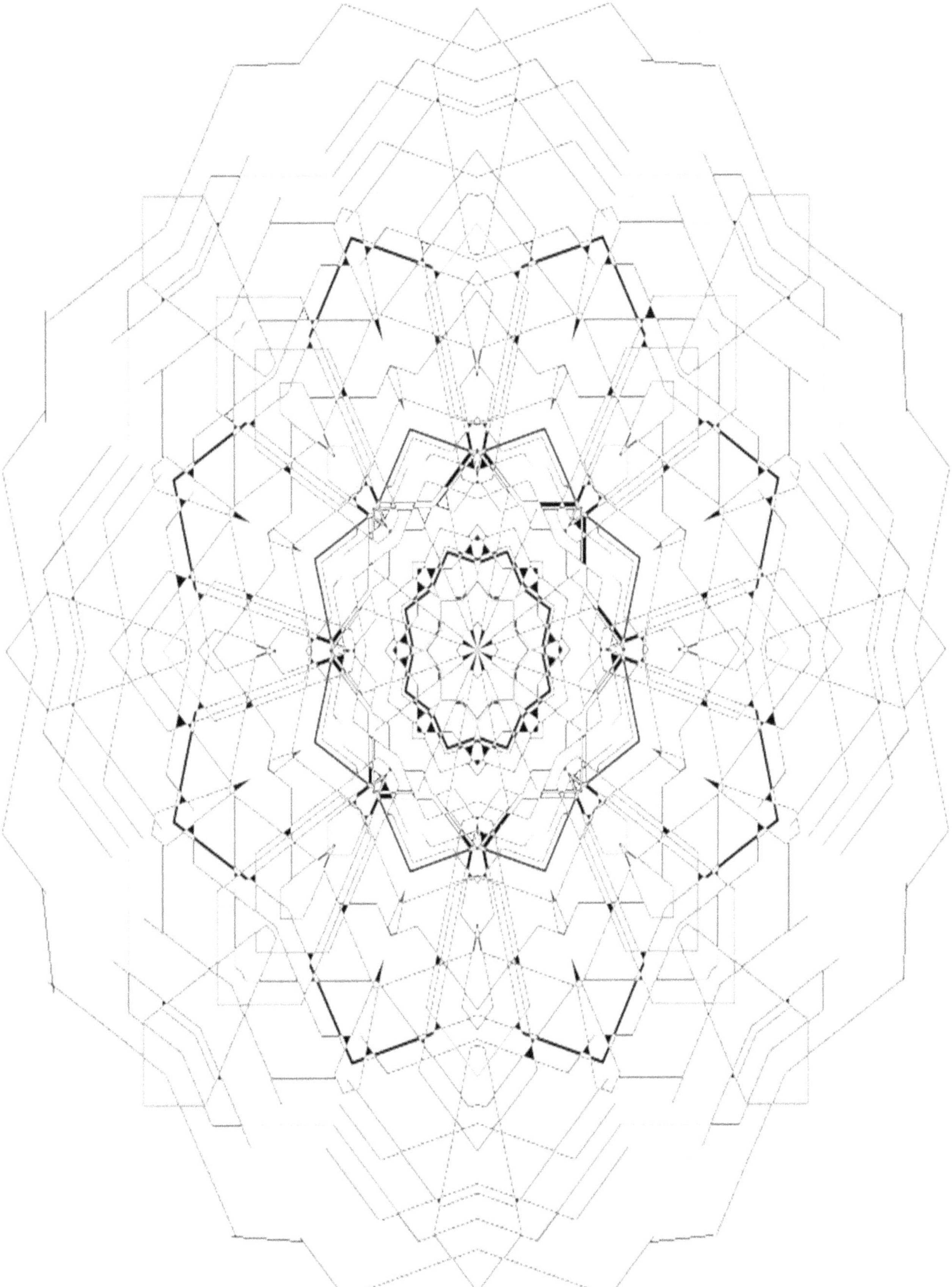

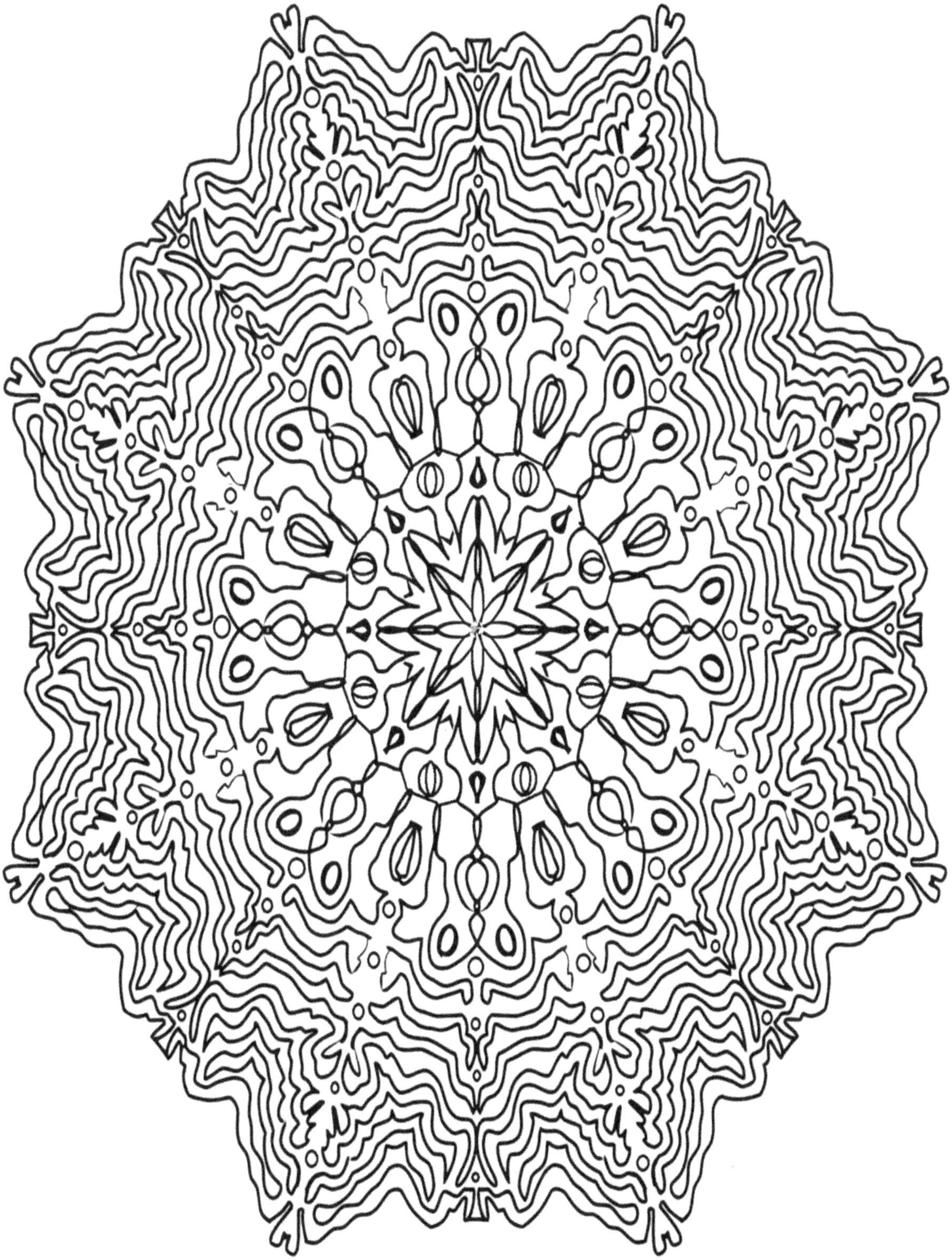

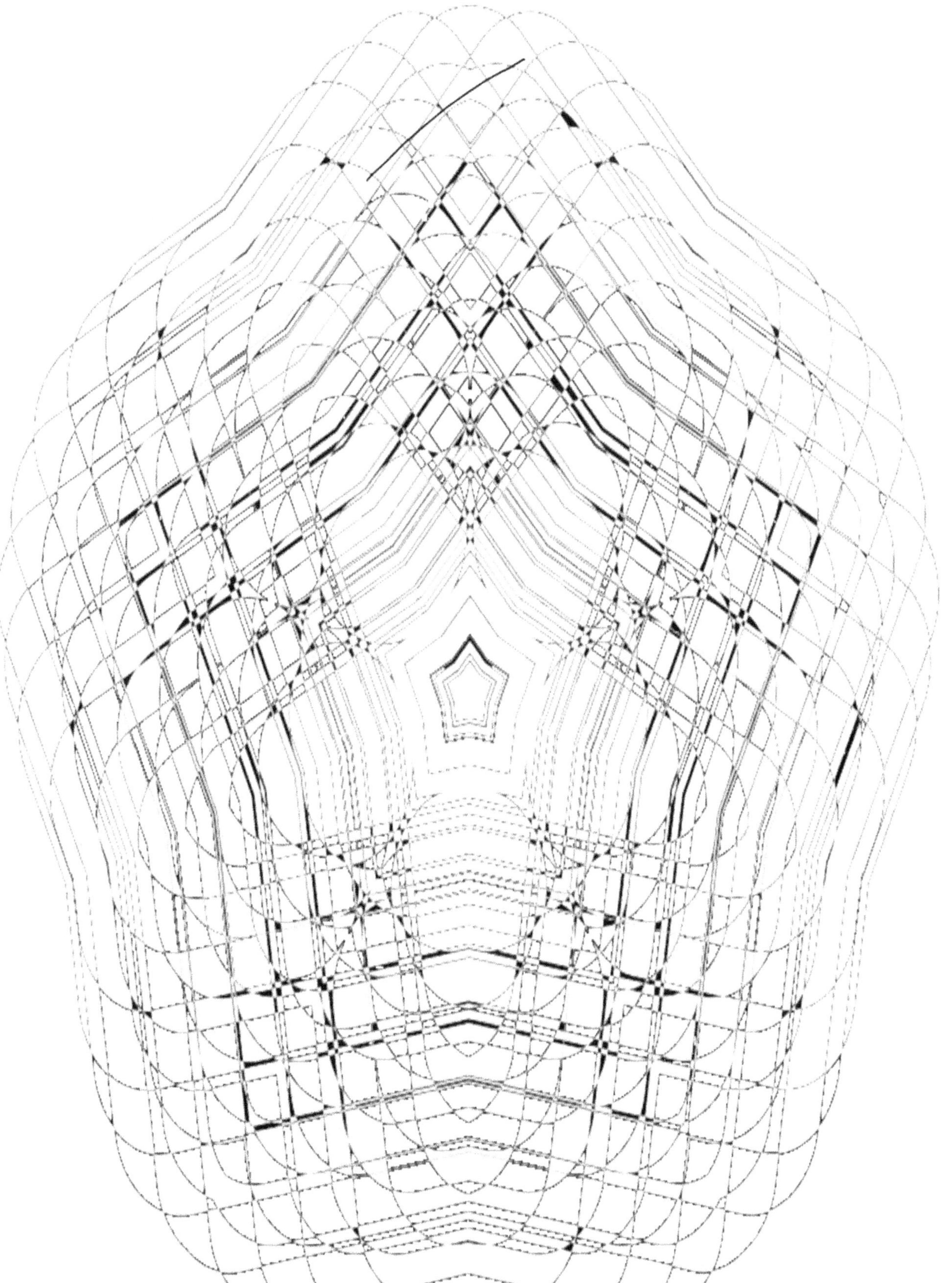

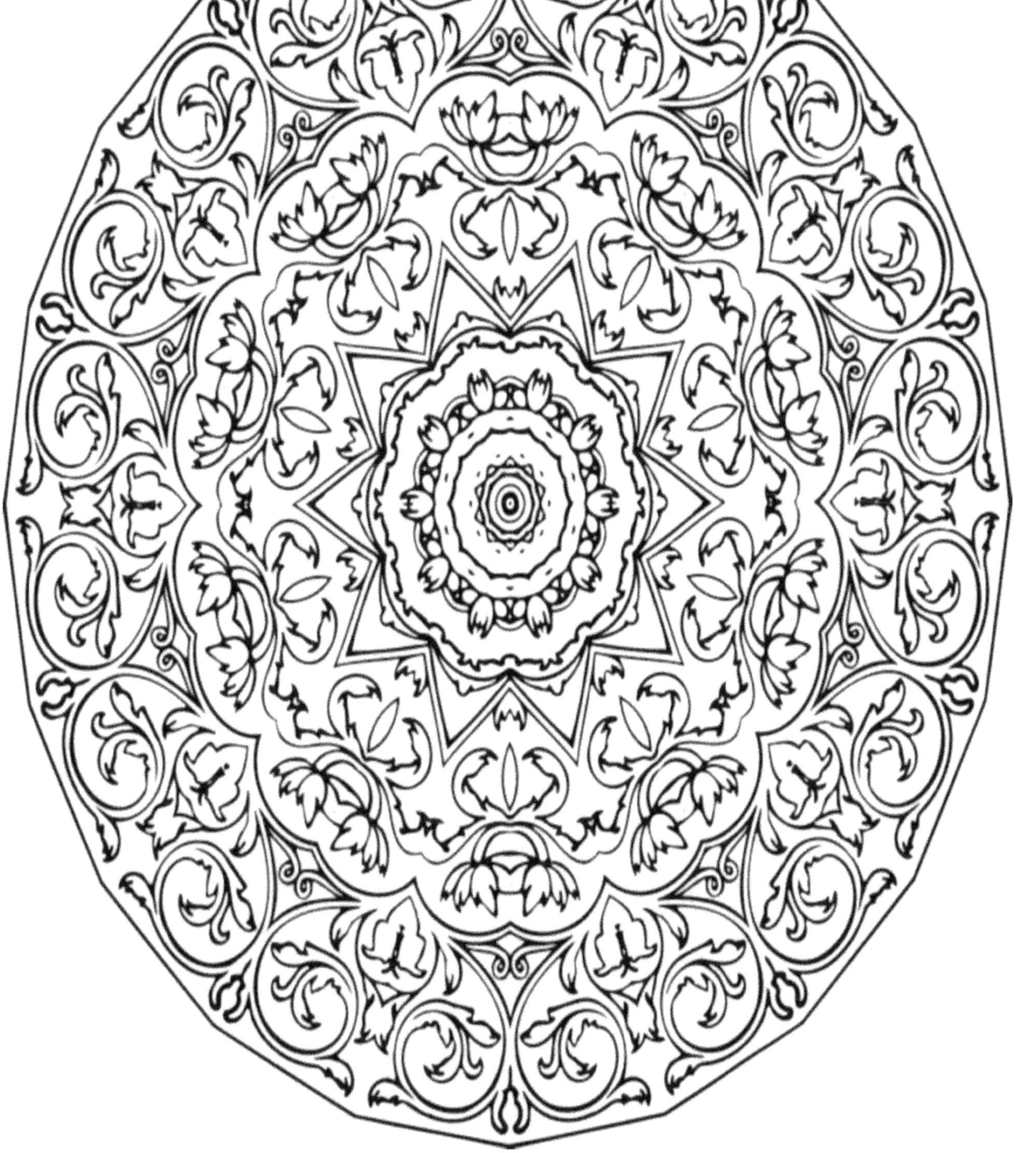

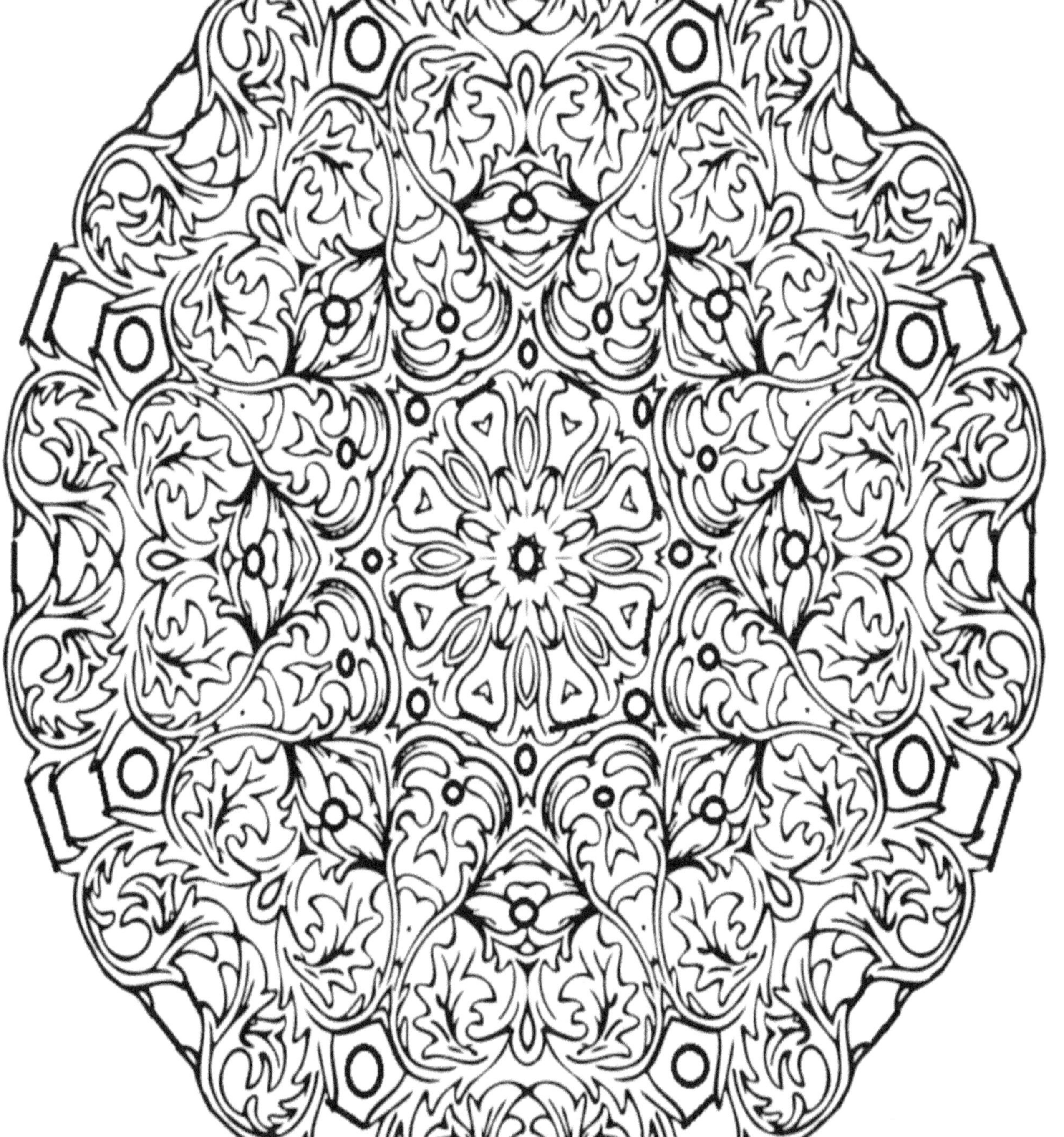

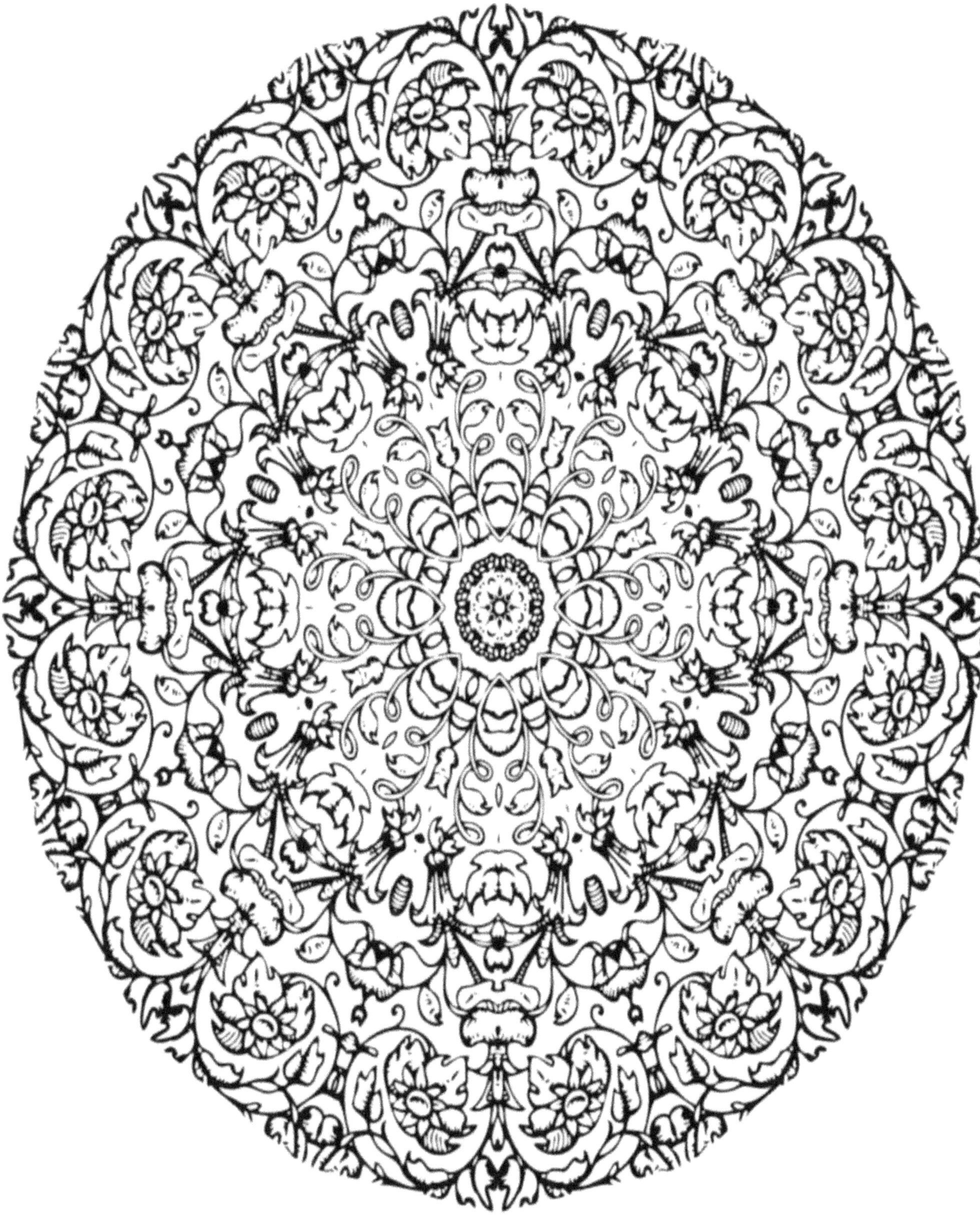

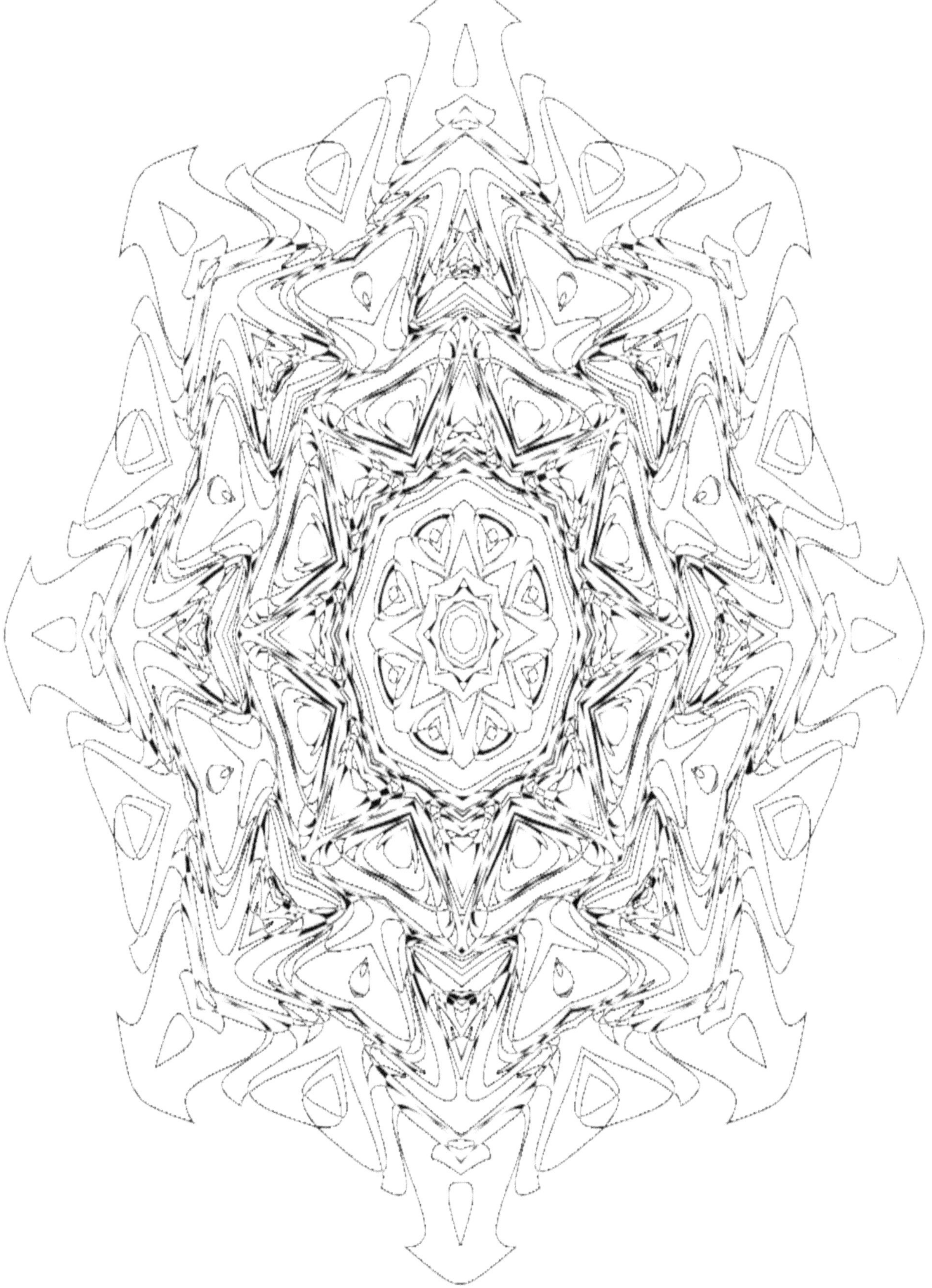

www.ingramcontent.com/pod-product-compliance
Lightning Source LLC
Chambersburg PA
CBHW081241280526
45787CB00006B/2757
* 9 7 8 1 5 2 0 1 3 7 4 1 4 *